Hindu Wedding: The Guide

यत्र नार्यस्तु पूज्यंते रमंते तत्र देवताः

Where women are honored, there the Gods delight

(Manusmrti 3-56)

Hindu Wedding: The Guide

Dr. A. V. Srinivasan

Foreword by Swami Anubhuvanandaji

White River Press
Amherst, Massachusetts

White River Press edition published November 2010

First published as *The Vedic Wedding* in a limited edition by
Periplus Line LLC, 2006.

White River Press
PO Box 3561
Amherst, MA 01004
www.whiteriverpress.com

Illustrations by Bapu

Printed in the United States of America

ISBN: 978-1-935052-38-8

The Publisher's Cataloging-In-Publication Data (prepared by The Donohue Group, Inc.,)
has catalogued the hardcover edition as follows:

Srinivasan, A.V.

The Vedic wedding : origins, tradition and practice : including a step-by-step wedding ceremony in Sanskrit with English transliteration and translation/ by A. V. Srinivasan ; illustrations by Bapu.

p. : ill., facsims. ; cm.

ISBN 0-9785443-0-7

1. Marriage service (Hinduism) 2. Marriage customs and rites, Hindu—History. I. Bapu, 1933- II. Title.

BL1226.82.M3 S65 2006

294.5/385

DEDICATION

The release of this book coincided with my daughter Sandhya's wedding.
This book is dedicated to Sandhya & Justin
and the couples shown below

KAVITA & JAMES
MONICA & PATRICK
THEANE & TEDDY
RACHNA & CHRISTOPHER
ANU & OSCAR
MEENA & MARK
RACHEL & ARUN
RAMYA & ERIC
KIMBERLY & RAM
DEEPA & ADAM
ANITA & RON
SHREYA & RAJEN
SHERENE & ROSS
SANDHYA & JUSTIN

शतमानं भवतु शतायुः पुरुषः
शतेंद्रियः आयुष्येवेंद्रिये प्रतितिष्ठति

May you be bestowed with a life of a hundred years, with senses a hundredfold virile
and may your longevity equal that of Indra himself.

FOREWORD
by
Swami Anubhavanandaji

The Hindu aim of ultimate emancipation from relative existence is attained by weeding out the individual "I". This goal can be attained through the marriage or union of a couple in a Vedic Ceremony. Keeping this in view, many traditions and practices are prescribed, from arranging a suitable match to the arrival of the bride in her new home. The Vedic marriage, popularly called the Hindu marriage, is designed to establish a close relationship of love and understanding not only between the partners but also between their families. Thus when a boy and girl get married they are opening a new chapter, expanding their "I" to include all the family members. This is achieved by conducting all the rituals related to the marriage ceremony as brought out by Dr. A.V. Srinivasan in his publication *Hindu Wedding*: *The Guide.*

The exhaustive treatment of this subject by Dr. Srinivasan in compiling all aspects of the mantras, their meaning and their importance, is praiseworthy. Credit goes to him for fulfilling the aspirations of the younger generation to know the meaning of the various rituals and the reasons why they are conducted. His experience in solemnizing trans-cultural marriages truly makes this publication universal.

This book deserves a special place in all libraries and in homes where married life is considered a means to attain freedom from day to day worries yet continues to provide a spiritual path. It is said that the "*Grhastha Ashram*" is the source of happiness both here and hereafter.

Swami Anubhavanandaji

Author's Note

The primary purpose of this book is to provide the complete text for a basic Hindu wedding ceremony. All the mantras, transliterations and translations given here are taken directly from the author's previous publication, *The Vedic Wedding: Origins, Tradition and Practice.*

"**The inspiration for this book** came from the young Indians in the United States who have approached me in the past three decades to seek my advice and to have me officiate at their weddings." (From the Author's Note, *The Vedic Wedding: Origins, Tradition and Practice.)*

The current book, **Hindu Wedding: The Guide,** includes all the elements needed to plan, coordinate and perform the ceremony itself.

The appendices include a form for family data essential for use in the rituals, a materials list, a sample program and a wide variety of additional pujas and ceremonies that may be of interest depending upon individual family traditions.

The CD containing all the mantras used in the ceremony may be ordered directly from: **www.cdbaby.com or www.periplusbooks.com.**

किंस्विन् मित्रं गृहेसतः भार्या मित्रं गृहेसतः
kimsvinmitram gr̥hēsata:? bhāryāmitram gr̥hēsata:
Who is the friend of a householder? A spouse

TABLE OF CONTENTS

I. Introduction 1

Hindu Philosophy of Marriage 1
Wedding and Marriage 3

II. Outline for the Wedding Ceremony

Basic Steps 4
Basic Steps, with Description 5

III. Preparations for the Wedding Ceremony

A. Planning 11
B. Pujas 17
C. Rehearsal 19

IV. The Wedding Day: Preliminaries

A. Arrangements at the Mantap 21
B. Bride's Family Prepares to Meet the Groom 25
C. The Baraat Arrives 27
D. Milni/Swagatam: Bride's Family Greets the Groom 28
E. The Groom is Escorted to the Mantap 30
F. Overview 31

V. The Vedic Ceremony

Preparatory Chants 38
Vara Puja & Sankalpam 44
Bride's Arrival & Garland Exchange 52
Hasta Milap & Pravara 56
Kanyadanam 58
Mangalyadharanam 63
Agni Pratishtapana 68
Homas: Pradhana Homa; Laja Homa 70
Saptapadi 82
Closing ceremonies:
Arati 87
Ashirvadam 89
Recessional 93

VI. Appendices

Appendix I: Materials 95
Appendix II: Rehearsal 104
Appendix III: Engagement; Yagnopavitam; Kashiyatra; Grhapravesham 107
Appendix IV: Additional Wedding Customs & Rituals 130
Appendix V: Vedic Calendar 151
Appendix VI: Bridal Attire 158
Appendix VII: Ganapati Puja; Gauri Puja 169
Glossary 199
Transliteration Scheme 208

Hindu Wedding: The Guide

भार्या दैव कृतः सखा

"A wife is a God-given friend"

I. Introduction

The Hindu Philosophy of Marriage

In the Aranya Parva of that great epic of the Hindus known as the Mahabharata, one of the 120 questions the Yaksha asked Yudhishtira was "*kimsvin mitram gr̥hesata:?*" i.e.Who is the friend of a householder? To which the prince answered "*bhāryā mitram gr̥hesata:*" i.e. the friend of a householder is his spouse. According to Hindus, therefore, the basis for marriage is friendship. According to Hindus, this friendship is the understanding, the promise and the commitment that unites a man and a woman. There is absolutely no question about the role of a woman, her importance, her position in this equation that binds them together.
The Hindu Marriage Act of 1955 passed by the Indian Parliament mandates that a Hindu marriage is considered legal only upon completion of the seventh step in the wedding rite known as Saptapadi, when the words spoken in Sanskrit by the groom to the bride declare:

सखा सप्तपदी भव
सख्यंते गमेयं
सख्यंते मायोशः
सख्यंते मायोश्टः

sakhā saptapadī bhava
sakhyamtē gamēyam
sakhyamtē māyōśa:
sakhyamtē māyōśta:

With these seven steps may you become my friend.
May I deserve your friendship.
May my friendship make me one with you.
May your friendship make you one with me.

Hindu ancestors went even further: they blessed the bride by saying:

मूर्धानं पत्युरारोह (*murdhānam patyurārōha*) meaning
"May your husband keep you on his head"
i.e. "Let him respect you".

Hindu religion and culture are rooted in the Vedas composed around 1500 B.C.E. or earlier. The Vedic ideal of marriage, according to Abhinash Chandra Bose (*The Call of the Vedas*, page 259, Bharatiya Vidya Bhavan, 1970), "is that of perfect monogamy, the life-long companionship of two people. This practice must have been well established, as is evident from the fact that the Vedic rishi seeking comparisons for perfect duality for the twin deities, the Ashvins, gives, along with examples of two eyes, two lips, etc. that of a married couple".

Wedding and Marriage

We shall start with the assumption that marriage is defined as the journey through life together of a loving, committed couple. Marriage is largely a social arrangement between two adults but is governed by laws of the land that offer protection to the essential individualities of the two persons so that the union may continue to be secure and peaceful. Through a solemn ceremony this social arrangement also procures a religious sanction which serves as an umbrella under which the commitments made can be preserved as long as the couple shall live.

A wedding, on the other hand, is an event and a ritual. It is the process that launches a couple into the institution known as marriage or, in religious terms, holy matrimony, and this process is therefore a social-cum-religious set of procedures defined by the cultural, religious and social heritages of the partners.

The Hindu wedding ceremony is based on Vedic traditions and rituals originating in the Rig Veda, the earliest of the four ancient Sanskrit books of knowledge which form the basis of Hinduism. Variations of procedures are to be found in the Yajur, Sama and Atharva Vedas, and the Grihya Sūtras (domestic rituals). Conjugal union has always been considered an important religious and social celebration, defining the beginning of the second stage of earthly existence, the first, beyond childhood, being that of the student. These rituals, which date back at least 5,000 years, form a dramatic sequence.

II. Outline for the Wedding Ceremony

A review of publications on wedding rites in modern Indian languages confirms the extent of variation dictated by geography and changing times. The question then is which steps to consider when planning a particular modern Hindu wedding.

Based on the Vedic sources and a desired framework of space and time, one may define the following basic steps as essential to satisfying most of the ritualistic needs of those raised in the Hindu faith.

Basic Steps:

- Swagat/ Swagatam or Milni: The meeting and greeting of both families.
- Vara Puja: Dialogue between the bride's father and the groom.
- Jayamala/Jai Mala: Exchange of garlands.
- Pravara: Announcement of lineage.
- Kanyadanam: Giving away the bride.
- Mangalyadharanam: Tying the mangalasutra.
- Agni/Homas: Fire rituals.
- Mangal Phera: Circling the fire.
- Saptapadi: Seven steps.
- Ashirvadam: Blessings.

A final program can be developed around this framework to suit individual family practice. Some steps may be omitted and some customary rituals added. A list of possible additional ceremonies follows in Appendices III and VII, as well as other traditional rites and customary practices in

Appendix IV listed in approximate order of usage during a wedding ceremony.

The names used for these rites may differ from one family to another. The couple may also wish to add such contemporary North American customs as vows or an exchange of rings.

Basic Steps with Description:

- **Swagat/ Swagatam or Milni**: The meeting and greeting of both families.

  Preliminary rites to this event can include one or more of the following: Ganesh Puja, Sehra Bandi (turban tying), or a Kashiyatra ceremony for the groom at an assembly of his relatives. There may also be a long or an abbreviated Baraat or joyous arrival of the groom, accompanied by relatives and music, riding, for example, a horse, a cart, a car, or on foot.

  At the Swagatam ceremony, the groom and his entourage are greeted at the door or gateway to the venue by the bride's parents, siblings, and other relatives, including at least five married ladies carrying fruit, flowers, deepa (lamp), dhoopa (incense), and new clothing if desired. The officiant blesses the groom, and prays for an obstacle-free ceremony.

  The bride's mother performs an arati, anointing him with a tilak, and akshata (turmeric-tinted raw rice), and sprinkling perfumed water.

The bride's father garlands him, and other male relatives on both sides garland each other. The groom may receive a sweet or sweet drink at this time (madhuparkam) from the bride's parent, or later from the bride.

The groom is then escorted to the mantap.

- **Vara Puja**: Dialogue between the bride's father and the groom.

Following the opening mantras to consecrate the water and offer prayers to a variety of Hindu gods, the bride's father declares his intention to give his daughter in marriage at this auspicious time, in this place (Sankalpam). He then welcomes the groom, and makes his offer of his daughter's hand in marriage. The groom accepts, and agrees to perform the wedding rites to become a householder, living within the constraints of dharma.

- **Jayamala/Jai Mala**: Exchange of garlands.

The bride arrives escorted by her maternal uncle(s), and/or aunts, sisters, cousins and friends. At this stage some families may raise a screen or Antarpat to block the groom's view of her approach. Rice or a mixture of sweet and bitter materials (Jeeriga Bellum) may be tossed over the screen by both before the screen is lowered. The bride garlands the groom, and is, in turn, garlanded by him. The bride's father places her right hand in the right hand of the groom (Hasta Milap).

❖ **Pravara:** Announcement of lineage.

A formal public announcement of the names of the bridegroom and the bride now follows in front of the assembled. In some traditions this step takes place earlier with some elaboration at the Swagatam when the Baraat arrives. The principals are introduced by declaring their lineage beginning with great-grandfather and proceeding with grandfather and father from both families. This serves as an opportunity to remember the ancestors on this auspicious occasion and seek their blessing. Traditionally the Pravara is recited three times, but can be done just once.

❖ **Kanyadanam:** Giving away the bride.

The bride's father repeats his intention to offer his daughter in marriage. The bride and groom face each other with the bride's cupped palms under the groom's, supporting the bride's father's cupped palms holding a coconut. The bride's mother pours consecrated water from a kalasha (traditional water urn) over the coconut while the priest or the bride's father chants mantras for the wellbeing of the bride in her new life.

❖ **Mangalyadharanam:** Tying the mangalasutra.

While the tying of the mangalasutra necklace around the bride's neck is very traditional to South Indian custom, it is common enough to other parts of India to be included as a basic step. The modern necklace is tied with a clasp or hook but, for the purpose of this ritual, may also be tied with 3 turmeric-tinted threads, first by the groom, followed by his mother and then by his sister. Some traditions still consider this to be the point at which the couple is declared married.

❖ **Agni/Homas**: Fire rituals.

Homa, or Havan, the fire ritual, is a crucial step among Hindu wedding rites. In orthodox families, when weddings were performed in a village in the bride's home, the fire from the bride's family's own domestic fire was kindled by the officiant or by the groom and, in some cases would be preserved to accompany the bride to her new home. The fire god, Agni, is considered to be not only the recipient of worship here, but also the priest, a witness acting as an intercedent between the new couple and the gods to whom the smoke of sacrifice ascends. During these rituals the couple makes offerings of samagris: ghee (clarified butter), grain, herbs, incense, sandalwood or a spice mixture, declaring that all their material possessions are indeed Agni's.

❖ **Mangal Phera**: Circling the fire. This rite is also called Laaja Homa.

The bridegroom holds the right hand of the bride while together they walk four times, sunwise, around the agni kunda (fire vessel) with garments knotted together (Gatha Bandan). The four rounds, or circumambulations are dedicated to the ideal of *chaturvidha phala purushaartha*, by which two vital aspects of life, *artha* (material) and *kāma* (emotional), are controlled by *dharma* (right conduct) in order to achieve *moksha* (salvation). The groom leads the bride for three rounds, sunwise, as he or the officiant chants the mantras. The fourth round, however, praying for moksha, is led by the bride. As they return to the starting point, after each round, they offer laja (puffed rice) to Agni. While a variety of puja materials (havan samagri) are offered in the primary fire ritual, during Laja Homa only parched/puffed rice is offered. The bride's brother (or a friend) positions himself to one side at the head of the kunda with a bowl of parched/puffed rice and fills the open palms of the bride with it at the end of each round. As the mantras are chanted by the groom or the priest in his behalf, the bride offers the contents to the fire while the groom offers a spoonful of ghee.

At the end of the fourth round, the bride may place her foot on a stone slab, symbolizing stability (Ashmarohana), after which the groom may place toe rings on the second toe of each foot. She may, at this point, also be directed to view the Pole Star (Dhruva Darshan), another symbol of stability or fidelity.

A number of family-based extra customary rites can be added here. These include: vows; ritual gifts of clothing and jewelry, especially bangles; rites to ward off adverse events; rites involving games of tossing of rice or flowers; an arati; special blessings for the bride by married women: "*Saubhagyavati Bhava*" (May you be fortune-favored).

- **Saptapadi**: Seven Steps.

Indian civil law recognizes the completion of the seven steps to be the climax of the ceremony and the finalization of the act of marriage. Each step specifies a separate blessing, for food, strength, austerity, love, welfare of cattle, prosperity, and sacred illumination.

Even this basic rite has different versions. One version prescribes that seven circles be drawn using rice flour to the north of the agni kunda and that the couple step into each circle holding hands, led by the bridegroom as the latter chants the appropriate verses. Again, the circles may be heaps of raw rice, or, in yet another version, seven lines are drawn in one large circle of rice and the bride places her right foot on one line after another. In some cases, as the groom recites the mantras, he bends down to hold, with his right hand, the right large toe of the bride to help her take each step. At each step he prays that Mahavishnu follow and bless the bride and grant the wishes stipulated in that step. Some parents recall circling the fire seven times. The confusion may be due to a shloka which refers to circles (mandala) which is intended to refer to the circles into which the bride and the groom step. The most popular and acceptable choice is for the bride and groom to take the seven steps together, holding hands, in one circumambulation around the fire.

- **Ashirvadam:** Blessings.

Seven chants of blessings are invoked for the couple as they stand together, in the names of many divine and legendary couples, as the audience chants *Tathastu*, “It shall be so” and sprinkles akshata (turmeric-tinted rice) on their heads. They may also seek blessings from elders in the family following this final step.

III. Preparations for the Ceremony

A: Planning

Planning for a wedding is a labor of love and worry. Some tasks are obvious: the need to design a guest list, and invitations, choose the immediate wedding principals (best man, bridesmaids), to decide what to wear, to decide the venue, the menu, the flowers, to book the photographer, the videographer, the music person. Some choices are clear while some might need a professional planner, or a very handy and knowledgeable relative, or a giant to-do file. All of these need time and money.

The traditional Indian wedding in North America has added all the above to a subplot: an elaborate ceremony of multiple rituals collected over thousands of years. In India itself the ceremony is the main event--chaotic but colorful, but chaotic. The chaos apparent to the outside world has little to do with the basic rites but with the many customs, social, family and regional, which have attached to this signal event in the lives of everyone involved.

How does a couple celebrate this event in a modern setting, often many miles away from their own homes, their parents' homes, or India, without losing the color, the joyous verve, the religious depth, the aroma, the sights and sounds of a real, traditional Indian wedding?

While much thought and preparation go into the kind of planning described in a hundred glossy magazines, another kind of plan is needed for the day of a Vedic wedding.

Very often this ceremony is under-planned and left to chance, wedged between photo sessions, between cocktails and dinner, and vulnerable to mishaps, puzzlement on the part of guests and new in-laws, and over-spending on materials.

This book recommends: a Family Data Form, a Materials List, a Music/Photographer/Videographer/Sound Guide, a Fire Management Plan for managing homas/havans, planning preliminary pujas and other rites, and a Rehearsal for basic steps in the wedding.

Family Data Form: see Appendix I. Wedding plan formats usually consist of lists of what to buy, where to get it, and what to pay. This suggested form allows for personal data which will be needed for the eve and the day of the ceremony, and names of individuals involved. The officiant will need this data. It can also be expanded for use by the couple in deciding which friends, relatives and other personnel will be directly involved in the wedding ceremony.

Vedic Wedding Materials List: see Appendix I. The list given here is basic, and will help reduce the need in cost and bulk.

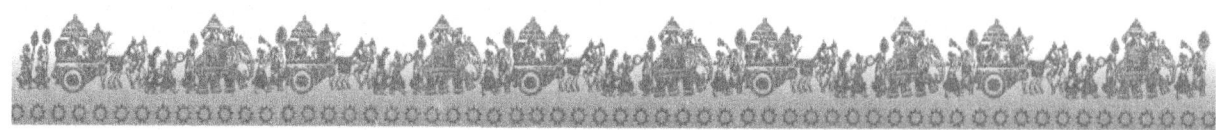

Fire Management: Fire ceremony materials are included in Appendix I. The central role of the fire ritual in the Hindu wedding rites cannot be emphasized enough. No Vedic ceremony is complete without an offering or oblation to Agni. Couples planning a wedding in a commercial venue need to know the rules concerning open flames. Since most hotels and wedding banquet establishments tolerate candles and lanterns/lamps as table décor, this should not be a problem.

The agni kunda or fire ceremony vessel is available from many sources. It could be a simple bronze hibachi, or a regular vessel rented along with the mantap and other typical wedding gear from an Indian event coordinator.

Whichever is used for the event, the couple should appoint two members of the wedding party to be in charge of the kunda. For complete safety, upon receiving a cue from the coordinator or officiant, the fire is lit and brought up to the mantap. It is best to assemble the kunda and the pedestal on which it sits ahead of time. The kunda may be covered in foil and placed on a table about 24" to 30" high topped with firebricks or tiles. A few pieces of dry wood sticks and a pinch of camphor may be placed inside the kunda. The whole assembly needs to be kept ready near the mantap. It is recommended that at the rehearsal or the day before the event, the men in charge practice lighting it up to test how to keep the flames neither too high nor too low. If the fire does go down too soon and begins to smoke, an additional pinch or two of camphor will restore the flame.

After the fire ceremonies are complete, and following the concluding Saptapadi step, it is best for the persons in charge to remove the fire vessel from the mantap and take it outside to be extinguished with a few handfuls of sand.

Historically when a wedding was conducted at the bride's home, the kunda and small amount of flame would be preserved for the new home's hearth fire. This of course is impractical and unnecessary in modern settings.

Also, it is recognized that a kunda in India would be lit with appropriate invocation at the beginning of the ceremony and maintained at the mantap throughout.

Music/ Sound Guide:
Joyful and appropriate music is an integral part of Hindu weddings and can be a great aid in structuring the flow of events into a delightful sequence. Whether the couple employs a deejay or a friend to coordinate and direct the output, a wide selection of music, live and on tape, is usually available for each stage of the ceremony.

Use of music during the religious rites:

- Before the rituals begin:

  festive nadaswaram or shenai, instrumental music on violin, mandolin, sitar or veena is appropriate while guests are being seated.

- For the arrival of the groom at the venue:

  vibrant music with drums (tabla, or mrdangam).

- As the bridegroom's party is greeted and brought to the mantap:

  festive nadaswaram or shehnai; or, rhythmic, loud Vedic chants.

- As the groom's entourage reaches the mantap:

  a Tyagaraja or other composition in praise of Mahaganapati.

- For the arrival of the bride:

  a melodious composition on the flute, such as Purandaradasa's "Bhagyaada lakshmi baaramma" (O prosperous Lakshmi, please do come).

Highlights for drumming and loud music:

Groom's arrival; the garlanding; the tying of the mangalsutra (wedding necklace); recessional.

Fill-in music for speaking gaps: low drumming or other instrumental music.

Live performances: It is hardly necessary to add that live performances by professionals, relatives and friends are always a welcome addition. This is especially true in cases where the bride wishes to change, as in some traditions, to clothes brought by her in-laws.

Many Indian wedding couples put aside an evening in advance for a Sangeet or full performance of professional music for their guests.

During a wedding there are many interludes when songs or even a short dance performance can fit in very well.

The basic recommendations may be summarized:

(1) It is recommended that the DJ attend the rehearsal, especially if not familiar with Vedic wedding practices.

(2) No silent gaps throughout the event, i.e. there shall always be music when there is no chanting and/or any other verbal action taking place at the mantap.

(3) The sound system should be thoroughly checked apriori.

(4) A clip-on microphone should be provided to the officiator.

The above suggestions help assure that things go pleasantly and smoothly from one step to the next in the ceremony, even when there are short unexpected delays. The right choice and sequence of music can keep an otherwise restive audience pleased, interested, involved and satisfied.

Photography/ Videography Guide:
Guidance and advice is needed for professional photographers and/or videographers covering the event, especially if they are not familiar with Hindu weddings. They need to have a coordinator provide them with the program, with a list of climactic moments and where to stand to get the correct view. They may also need a contact person to ask for names and explanations. The list of highlights and important steps given above for the deejay or music coordinator may be helpful.

Hindu wedding ceremonies are more complex than the average church or synagogue event. They involve more participants than the officiator and 2 principals, and more ritual objects than 2 finger rings. To begin with, there are two equally important processionals to be covered, that of the bridegroom as well as the bride. Once the principals are within the mantap, there is a steady stream of activities to be viewed and covered. Photographers and/or videographers will benefit from a clear, even marked-up program given to them ahead of time and a contact person, not otherwise engaged, to explain what is about to happen or what has just happened. The contact should be introduced to the photographer/videographer and stay available only as needed.

Preparations for the Ceremony

B: PUJAS

Family Pujas:

It is not uncommon for the immediate families to gather in their own homes or suites and have the bride and groom perform a major puja to their ishtadevata (preferred deity) or to Lord Satyanarayana before the wedding ceremony. Some may choose to visit a local temple and have a special puja performed there. A puja may also be performed near or at the location of the wedding. These are best done the day or night before.

Ganesh and Gauri Pujas:

Pujas to Mahaganapati (Ganesha) and Maheshwara (Shiva) are generally chosen by the groom's family and Gauri Puja by the bride's family. Again this depends upon family tradition. These pujas are usually performed, by or under the direction of a priest, by the bride and the groom, separately in their own quarters with their immediate families and friends attending.

It is quite adequate to perform these pujas by offering shodashopacharas (invocation, respectful greeting and prayer steps) in a brief format. (See Appendix VII: Pujas)

Normally each of these pujas should take about an hour using the materials, plans and procedures recommended in the reference. The chanting of the ashtothara (108 names of the deity being worshipped) and Mantrapushpa are appropriate before the concluding arati, followed by blessings from the assembled elders. Many families have expressed their feeling that performing and participating in these worship services helped reduce stress and brought about a sense of peace. Thus some time devoted to this activity prior to the wedding may help in more sense than one.

The materials and other ritual arrangements used at the pujas may be brought to the mantap later for use during the processionals and the main ceremony. (See Appendix I: Materials)

Preparations for the Ceremony

C. Rehearsal

A rehearsal is unheard of in Hindu weddings. It is mandatory in Western practice. Over the years we have found that the second generation growing up in North America, having previously observed or participated in the Christian or Jewish weddings of their friends, are puzzled at what sometimes appears to be a chaotic scene at Hindu weddings. When young Indians visit India and attend weddings, they report being shocked as they observe some rituals taking place on a stage with the immediate family surrounding the scene of action and milling around the stage, fetching this and conveying that, while the audience engages in multiple conversations among themselves and waits for the thing to end. Blaring music to which no one pays attention, a fully functioning kitchen that serves something as needed, and a blatant lack of involvement are all accepted as fun; perhaps it may be. This has been the author's experience also.

But we strongly believe that the beauty and grandeur of the scriptural mandates and the ceremonies are too important to ignore on a day which is so special to the principals. Therefore we have developed a format that has established without doubt that we can integrate discipline with joy and thus the sanctity of the samskara (Hindu rite of passage: here, the householder) can indeed be preserved.

To that end we strongly recommend a rehearsal in which a talk-through and a walk-through pertaining to the main steps can take place. This allows all those participants in the ceremonies the following day to indeed understand their individual roles, the sequence of the steps and the meaning of each ritual. Obviously, actual garlanding and homas do not take place during the rehearsal.

Again experience here has shown, with a well coordinated rehearsal, how enjoyable and successful the wedding can be. It has also shown how necessary items may be forgotten sometimes and events can get off-track when the rehearsal was either skipped, cut short, or principal helpers were absent. But there is no question about the value of this strategy and therefore we highly recommend it. There has generally been complete understanding of this need on the part of the families even when both are of the Hindu faith. (See Appendix II: Rehearsal)

IV. THE WEDDING DAY: Preliminaries

A. Arrangements at the Mantap;

B. The Bride's Family Prepares to Meet the Groom;

C. The Baraat Arrives;

D. Milni/Swagatam: The Bride's Family Greets the Groom;

E. The Groom is Escorted to the Mantap;

F. Overview.

A. The Mantap

The arrangement of the mantap, the sacred space, can vary from extremely simple to a very elaborately decorated wood or metal structure with posts, garlands and cloth or ceiling covered with Indian motifs. Some use the traditional four pillars or even flower stands to define a rectangular space, some have used gazebos available on the premises and decorated them with flowers. Any of these will do as long as the space is made special and distinct. Many services are also available to supply authentic mantaps. Outdoor mantaps need to be firmly anchored, especially when the ceremony is held on a beach.

Organization of materials at the mantap for greeting the bridegroom is illustrated below as a schematic.

Mantap Arrangement Schematic

Size about 20’ x 16’ generally facing east

Steps from both sides, firm and easy to use

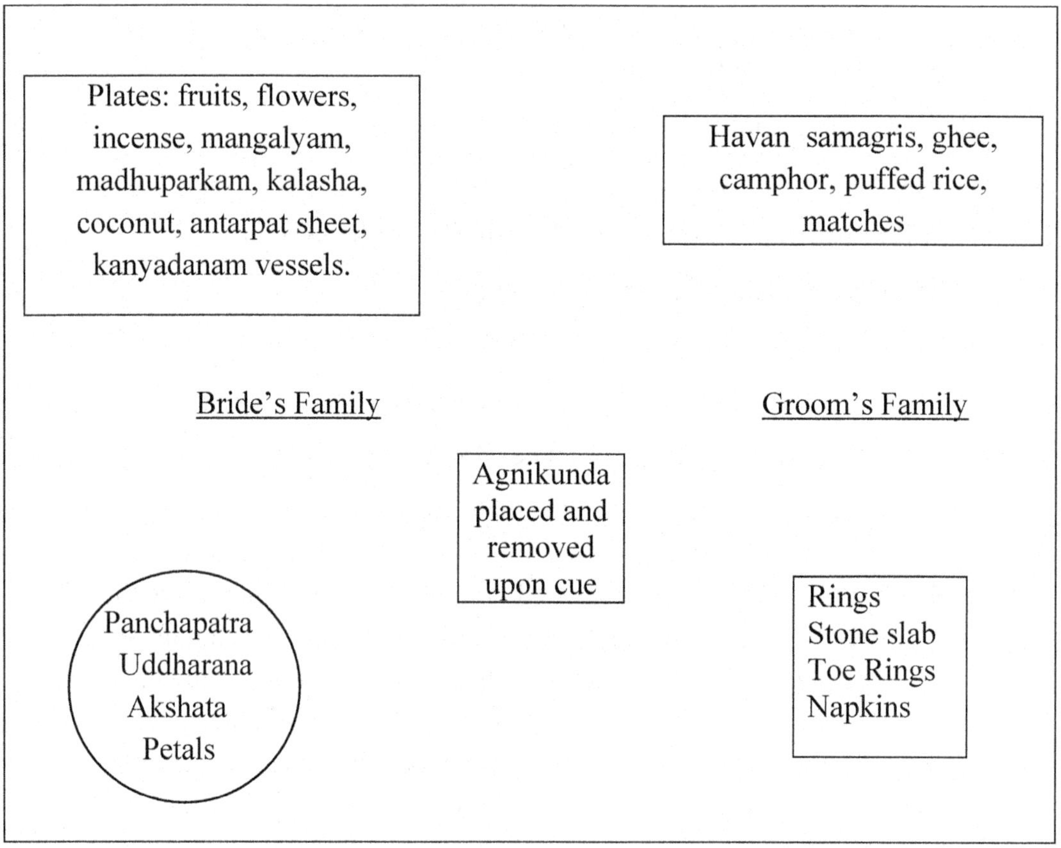

Audience

Recommended Arrangement of Materials

- **Seven (7) metallic plates** containing

5 types of fruit, (b) ceremonial cup of water, uddharana (ceremonial spoon), madhuparkam, kumkum, haldi and akshata, (c) flowers, (d) deepa, (e) agarbatti, perfumes, (f) the garland for the bridegroom and (g) kalasha on a bed of raw rice, filled to about a third with water, topped with a decorated coconut on a bed of leaves (mango or other fruit tree leaves). These should be placed at the front of the mantap in a row and ready to be picked up when the processional to receive the bridegroom starts.

For the bride's processional:

- Note: Some of these above plates (fruits, flowers) can be conveyed to the bride's quarters, after the groom's arrival, to be used in her processional and placed again on a table on the mantap later after her arrival. The only additional plates that will accompany the bride are (a) a plate with the mangalasutra on a silk cloth with a few petals of flowers, kumkum, haldi and few grains of akshata and (b) a garland for the bridegroom. Bridesmaids may carry additional flowers and deepas (lamps).

For use at the mantap:

- **A table for materials on the side of the mantap** towards the back is needed to place the plates described above upon return to the mantap after bringing the bridegroom in the processional. Also: the sheet/saree to be used as antarpat; an extra container with water; a coconut; and a basin to collect water poured during the Kanyadanam ceremony.

- **A second table inside the mantap with materials for the use of the officiator**, with:
  (1) a plate of flowers or flower petals
  (2) a plate with small cups of kumkum, haldi
  (3) a bowl of akshata
  (4) pancha patra with uddharana (spoon)
  (5) a silver or copper vessel with water

- **A third table for havan materials on the other side of the mantap:** (1) four small cups of puffed rice, (2) small jar of ghee with a spoon, (3) few small sticks of wood about 2 to 3 inches long, (4) camphor); (5) an extra bowl of akshata

- **Havan kund (fire receptacle), with a small table to hold it,** with (1) havan samagri (mixture for offering), (2) small wood sticks or twigs, (3) cube(s) of fire-starter, (4) four or five tablets of camphor, (5) candle stub, (6) matches or lighter.

- A fire extinguisher and/or a small bucket of sand (in the vicinity, but out of obvious sight).

It is best to have all the plates arranged before they are brought to the site. It is important that the entire mantap along with tables as described above be in place and checked out at least thirty minutes before the ceremony begins, that is, before going to meet the groom.

Entering and Exiting the Mantap:

The mantap is sacred space and no shoes can be worn within it once the sanctification ceremony begins. The mantap should be easily accessed when the groom's party, and later the bride's, arrives to enter. A chair may be needed for use by the bride and her entourage to remove shoes gracefully before they mount the mantap.

B. The Bride's Family Prepares to Meet the Groom

An assembly is formed at the mantap from among the bride's family (minus the bride) with the bride's parents, five ladies selected from the family, and the officiating priest. Each carries a plate as described below:

Materials for the Swagatam:

Bride's father: A garland in a plate; a friend or brother can assist with the plate when the time comes to garland the groom.
Bride's mother: plate with a lamp (deepa), petals, madhuparkam in a small cup, kumkum and haldi in containers.
Other greeters: each of five ladies carries a plate that may consist of fruits or flowers, agarbattis and perfume sprinkler, lamps and a copper or silver vessel with water and decorated coconut.
The priest: a plate with akshata, a panchapatra (a silver or copper bowl used in rituals) with water, and uddharana (ceremonial spoon).

Leaving to meet the groom:

At the moment appointed for the beginning of the ceremony, two or more rows of the processional are formed with the priest at the front row center, the bride's mother on one side and the father on the other side. The five ladies (other family members and friends may also join in) form the second and third rows. As nadaswaram, shehnai or any other form of selected music begins to play, the assembly proceeds towards the previously designated place where the bridegroom's party is met. The point of Milni (meeting) is a decorated entrance or archway.

The timings should be such that the bride's party arrives at the meeting place a few moments before the groom's party reaches there.

C. The Baraat Arrives

It is customary for the bridegroom's family to assemble off-site before beginning the procession to be greeted later by the bride's family. Depending on the tradition, a choice is made by family and friends to have the groom ride a decorated animal (usually a horse) or a decorated vehicle (usually a convertible) and process towards the wedding hall in order to arrive at the previously agreed point where the other family's principals and the priest wait. This procession is usually quite lively with loud music and especially folk dance, and results in an appropriately joyous and festive mood.

Depending upon the families such a procession may take a few minutes to as long as half an hour or more. It is important to designate a person to keep track of the time so that the party is at the designated place at the appointed hour.

Timing of the steps in the ceremony may be set back if there is delay in this clearly free-for-all event. It is therefore best for the designated person to make an announcement, ten minutes before the main ceremony begins, requesting that the guests proceed to the wedding hall and take their seats.

Also it is helpful to have ushers hand out the program note and guide the guests to their seats to help keep the pace. It is best to direct the groom's guests to the right side of the mantap (from the audience vantage) and the bride's guests to the left side. A subtle requirement is that the bride's side arrives just a few seconds before the bridegroom's side arrives to adhere to the protocol of greeters.

If the families decide to have the groom proceed on a Kashiyatra, then the bride's party interrupts the "journey." In this case the priest addresses the groom and a dialogue ensues (See Appendix III: Kashiyatra). Following this rite, the ritual of greeting continues.

D. Milni/ Swagatam: The Bride's Family Greets the Groom

Upon arrival of the groom and his family at the pre-determined meeting point (Milni), the priest blesses the groom by sprinkling a few grains of akshata on his bowed head and chants:

शुक्लांबरधरं विष्णुं शशिवर्णं चतुर्भुजं
प्रसन्न वदनं ध्यायेत् सर्व विघ्नोप शांतये

śuklāmbaradharam viṣṇum śaśivarṇam caturbhujam
prasanna vadanam dhyāyēt sarva vighnōpa śāntayē

I meditate on Vishnu clothed in white, the color of the moon,
four-armed, of pleasant aspect, so that all obstacles may be lessened.

वक्रतुंड महाकाय सूर्यकोटि समप्रभा
निर्विघ्नं कुरु मेदेव सर्व कार्येशु सर्वदा

vakratunda mahaakāya sūryakōti samaprabhā
nirvighnam kuru mēdēva sarva kāryēśu sarvadā

Lord with curved tusk, immense presence,
and brilliance that matches a million suns, please remove
all obstacles in all my undertakings always.

The priest concludes the blessings by saying: "*avighnamastu* (May there be no obstacles)."

He then directs the bride's mother to apply a tilak, an auspicious mark of red powder (kumkum) to the forehead of the groom. She will then perform an arati, a blessing, by waving the plate with lit lamp clockwise three times in front of the groom. The bride's father garlands the groom and shakes his hand. If there is a perfume sprinkler on one of the plates, it is customary to sprinkle a few drops generally in the direction of the groom and his party.

At this point some families use the Milni as the occasion to garland some previously selected family members from each side. Upon completion of this formality, the bride's welcoming group turns around, proceeding towards the mantap with the groom at the center now flanked by both sets of parents and the priest and followed by the rest of the party.

E. The Groom is escorted to the Mantap

Placement at the mantap:

The processional reaches the mantap and the principals (priest, bridegroom and his parents, bride's parents or other elders in charge of bestowal and any other family members previously agreed to) ascend the platform and face the assembly. It is best to assemble the bridegroom and his parents (standing or sitting) on the right side of the mantap (vantage point of the audience) and the bride's parents on the left. The latter is the side from which the bride will enter the mantap. This is important because after the Mangalyadharanam (or similar defining step) the bride is traditionally asked to move to the left of the groom and stay there for the rest of the ceremony.

Groomsmen may stay on the mantap if they wish and if there is space. Otherwise they may be seated nearby. While some may still be ushering guests at this point, they may soon be needed to help with Antarpat or fire preparation.

Other family members may remain at the mantap, either seated at the edge, or as available to help. Friends and family members who are designated to help at the mantap may also have reserved seats in the front or may prefer to stand at the designated location.

When everyone is settled it is recommended that the officiant or another coordinator or greeter give an overview of the ceremony to follow.

This can serve as a cue for the bride's party to get ready to approach close enough to the entrance but not within sight of the mantap, and wait for the final signal to begin their own processional entrance.

F. Wedding Overview

The overview concept suggested here was developed by the author over the years and used in about thirty weddings. It works very well. The concept replaces the need to stop the ceremony often to "describe" each step before or after it is taken, so that the flow of the process is smooth. Generally we have found the audience in the ceremonies we have conducted to be alert, curious and fully capable of absorbing the spirit and meaning of the procedures as long as they are given a broad background and philosophy of the rituals. With an overview of the type shown below and a program note in hand, the assembled guests can follow the dynamics of the wedding process very well.

Author's Overview: The following is the general overview that the author has used with minor modifications and which may be used as a basis by another officiant with his or her own embellishments:

Good afternoon! My name is Srinivasan and in behalf of the two families that are about to be united through the solemn ceremony of a wedding, it is a pleasure for me to welcome all of you to participate in the ceremonies.

For the benefit of those in the audience who may be new to our Vedic wedding rites, I would like to give a brief overview of the several steps the two young persons are about to take. The program you have received is a condensed version of the procedures and you may wish to refer to it from time to time.

The Hindu wedding ceremony is based on Vedic traditions and rituals originating in the Rig Veda, the earliest of the four ancient Sanskrit books of knowledge which form the basis of Hinduism.

Our ancestors set up guidelines to make sure that this institution known as marriage is a permanent one capable of not only bringing happiness to two young people, but also providing a delicate balance so that the new family enjoys the fullness of life within the framework of what we call dharma, the Hindu code of right conduct. Dharma is one of the four aspects of life that Hindus strive to live for. The other three are artha and kama, which underline the financial/practical and the emotional aspects, and the final goal is liberation or moksha. All the rituals that comprise the wedding ceremony, directly or indirectly charge the couple to strive for these four aspects, known as **चतुर्विध फल पुरुषार्थ** (*caturvidha phala puruṣārtha*). As you will see, we have successfully preserved the principal elements and spirit of the traditional wedding program which, in the not-too-distant past, took as many as five days. The rituals, which date back at least 5,000 years, form a significant dramatic sequence.

We begin our ceremonies with a Vedic chant of benediction. The Vedic chant ends with a prayer for peace. The traditional seven Great Rivers of India are then invoked, because one of the principal elements in Hindu ritual is water. We have also chosen to include important river systems of the United States. Obviously if the wedding is held in another country, the river systems of that nation are invoked. The invocation is followed by a purification chant.

The groom has been received and honored by the bride's family. The sacred space, the mantap, has been prepared. We will locate and declare this time and space and invoke the principal Hindu Gods.

In just a couple of minutes, after the formal greetings, I shall instruct the bride's father and request him to declare his intention to honor the groom and his family, and to give away the bride to the trust and care of the bridegroom's family at this moment in time and space as specified. We will then receive the bride and her entourage accompanied by some members of her immediate family.

These initial steps pave the way for a ceremony known as kanyadanam, the ritual equivalent of leaving one family and setting the stage for the new family to establish its own home and thus begin a new life.

As with many world traditions, Hindu tradition also assumes that as an assembly of family and friends, you have acquired a special, although temporary, authority to grant permission when sought and offer blessings at appropriate intervals. Both these are granted by your free and firm declaration of a single word in Sanskrit **तथास्तु** (*tathāsthu*), meaning "It shall be so." When I seek such permission through words such as **अनुगृण्हंतु** (*anugr̥nhantu*) or **अधिब्रुवंतु** (*adhibruvantu*), please respond by saying, **तथास्तु** (*tathāsthu*).

I shall occasionally remind you of this sacred authority and it is therefore essential that you remain alert until the ceremony is complete.

The principal seal or bond between the bridegroom and the bride is a golden necklace, the mangalasutra, which the bridegroom places around the bride's neck. This particular necklace first receives the blessings of the elders in the two families, and it is the power of that blessing that we believe will sustain this couple for all time.

The latter ceremony known as Mangalyadharanam मांगल्य धारणं (*māngalyadhāraṇam*) is of deep significance. It begins with an invocation to all the Hindu Gods and Goddesses and, as I recite a chant of blessing, with an intense sound of music in the background, the bridegroom offers the necklace and puts it around the neck of the bride. This ceremony indeed is considered the climax in the series of steps. The couple is then declared husband and wife for all time.

It is an ancient practice of Hindus to invoke Agni, Fire, and the purifier of all, to serve as witness to the wedding vows. Holding hands, and with fire as witness, the couple pledge their love to each other and initiate a new domestic hearth.

Into the fire symbolic sacrifices through offerings of grain, herbs, clarified butter, incense, and sandalwood are made in a gesture of gratitude and worship to the gods and symbolizing the offer of all their worldly possessions to God's grace. Initially, the couple goes around Agni four times. The first three rounds led by the bridegroom signify the pledge to adhere to the practice of *dharma*, *artha* and *kama* but in the final round, the bride leads the bridegroom confirming the Hindu belief that salvation is impossible without the leadership of the lady of the house or the धर्मपत्नि (*dharmapatni*). Mutual wishes for prosperity, for children and for a long, happy life together follow in a series of ceremonial offerings to the fire.

This is followed by a ceremony called सप्तपदि (*saptapadi*) in which the couple take seven steps together in front of Agni, and pledge to each other their eternal friendship. The friendship element is important in our weddings, and signifies the nature of the promise and the commitment that bind a couple. This seventh step is also the event which makes the marriage legal in Indian law.

We will then ask you to witness this wedding and bless the couple with long life and prosperity, and again your approval will be sought.

We are ready to begin and we urge you to relax, enjoy the ceremonies and help us through the process.

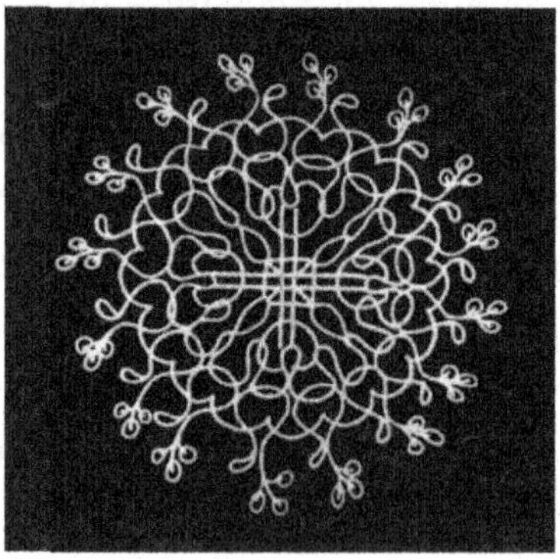

V. THE WEDDING CEREMONY

Invocation/Veda Mantras
Prayers/Salutations
Sankalpam
Vara Puja
Antarpat
Jayamala
Hasta Milap
Kanyadanam
Mangalyadharanam
Pradhana Homa
Mangal Phera/Laja Homa
Saptapadi
Ashirvadam/Blessings

<table>
<tr>
<td>

Invocation/Veda Mantras

The priest begins with the invocation which forms the first verse of the first chapter of Part One of the *Taittiriya Upanishad:*

Salutations to the assembly:

Chanting led by priest

</td>
<td>

ओं शं नो मित्रः शं वरुणः
शं नो भवत्वर्यमा
शं न इंद्रो
बृहस्पतिः
शं नो विष्णुरुरुक्रमः
नमो ब्रह्मणे
नमस्ते वायो
त्वमेव प्रत्यक्षं ब्रह्मासि
त्वामेव प्रत्यक्षं ब्रह्म वदिष्यामि
ऋतं वदिष्यामि
सत्यं वदिष्यामि
तन्मामवतु
तद्वक्तारमवतु
अवतु माम्
अवतु वक्तारं
ओं शांतिः शांतिः शांतिः

ओं नमस्सदसे नमस्पदस स्पतये
नमस्सखीनां पुरोगाणां चक्षुषे
नमोदिवे नमः पृथिव्यै
सप्रथसभांमे गोपाय
येचस्सभ्या स्सभासदः
तानिंद्रियावतः कुरु
सर्वमायुरुपा सतां
सर्वेभ्यो महांतेभ्यो नमो नमः

</td>
</tr>
</table>

ōm śam nō mitra: śam varuṇa: *śam nō bhavatvaryamā* *śam na indrō bṛhaspati:* *śam nō viṣṇururukrama:* *namō brahmaṇē* *namastē vāyō* *tvamēva pratyakṣam brahmāsi* *tvāmēva pratyakṣam brahma* *vadishyāmi* *ṛtam vadiṣyāmi* *satyam vadiṣyāmi* *tanmāvavatu* *tadvaktāramavatu* *avatu mām* *avatu vaktāram* *ōm shānti: shānti: shānti:*	OM, may the sun god Mitra and other Vedic gods–Varuna, Aryama, Indra, Brhaspati and the all pervading Mahavishnu–and all the devatas shower their blessings upon us. Salutations to Brahma, salutations to Vayu. You are a personification of Brahma. I shall proclaim you as Brahma. I shall always abide by dharma. I shall always speak the truth. May THAT protect us all (the preceptor and the disciple). OM peace, peace, peace!
ōm nama:ssadasē namaspadasa spatayē *nama:ssakhīnām purōgāṇām chakshuṣē* *namōdivē nama: pṛthivyai* *saprathasabhāmmē gōpāya* *yēchasabhyā ssabhāsada:* *tānindriyāvata: kuru* *sarvamāyurūpā satām* *sarvēbhyō mahānto: namō nama:*	Salutations to the assembly and its leader (presider), friends, family and other leaders present here. Salutations to heaven and earth. May all the honorable and powerful belonging to the family (present or absent) in this assembly be blessed with long life and be protected.

Invocation of the seven sacred rivers of India/America As the officiator chants the shloka invoking the sacred rivers, the bride's mother is instructed to pick up a vessel (usually a decorative one) and pour water from it in the form of a thin stream into another vessel (usually smaller) until the latter is nearly full. An uddharana (a decorative, ceremonial spoon) is slipped into the latter ready for use during the service. Similarly rivers of North America may also be invoked by including major river systems in the United States through the shloka shown here.	गंगेच यमुनेचैव गोदावरी सरस्वति नर्मदा सिंधु कावेरि जलेस्मिन् सन्निधिं कुरु  कोलंबिया कोलराडो चैव मिस्सौरि मिसिसिप्पी रियोग्रांडी च हड्संच कनेटिकट् नदीनां जलेः अस्मिन् सन्निधिं कुरु
Purification/Shuddhi As the officiator offers a spoonful of the sanctified water into the open palms of the principals on the stage, the individuals simply wipe their palms with it.	अपवित्रः पवित्रोवा सर्वावस्थां गतोपिवा यस्मरेत् पुन्डरीकाक्षं बाह्याभ्यंतरः शुचिः
Pranayama/Gayatri Pranayama is an essential chant in Vedic rituals and is meditated as air is drawn in through one nostril and ejected slowly through the other. It is advisable for the officiator and/or the bride's father to recite the chant.	प्राणायाम ओं भूः ओं भुवः ओं सुवः ओं महः ओं जनः ओं तपः ओगुं सत्यं ओं तत्सवितुर्वरेण्यं भर्गो देवस्य धीमहि, धीयोयोनः प्रचोदयात् ओं आपो ज्योतिरसो अमृतं ब्रह्म ओं भूर्भुवस्सुवरों

gangēca yamunēcaiva gōdāvarī saraswati narmadā sindhu kāvēri jalē:smin sannidhim kuru *kolambiyā kolarāḍō caiva missauri misisippī riyōgrānḍī ca haḍsanca kanetikat nadīnām jalē:smin sannidhim kuru* *apavitra: pavitrōvā sarvāvasthām gatōpivā ya:smarēt punḍarīkākṣam bāhyābhyantara śśuchi:*	O waters of Ganga, Yamuna, Godavari, Saraswati, Narmada, Sindhu, Kaveri, manifest yourselves here. May the sacred waters of Columbia, Missouri, Mississippi, Rio Grande, Hudson and Connecticut rivers manifest themselves here. Impure or pure and whatever your state of mind may be, you shall attain purity both inward and outward by mere remembrance of Pundarikaksha (the lotus-eyed, i.e. Vishnu)
prāṇāyāma *ōm bhū: ōm bhuva: ōm suva: ōm maha: ōm jana: ōm tapa: ōgum satyam ōm tatsaviturvvarēṇyam bhargō dēvasya dhīmahi, dhīyōyōna: prachōdayāt ōm āpō jyotirasō amṛtam brahma ōm bhūrbhuvassuvarōm*	**Pranayama** Om. That which pervades earth, sky and heaven, which is worthy of worship, that has no beginning; that which is the light of wisdom and truth; Let us meditate on the radiance of that divinity. May that brilliance help inspire and illuminate our minds. That One which represents water, light and is the quintessence in all things; May that almighty spirit pervading the earth, atmosphere, and heaven bless us with enlightenment. *(after Sant Keshavadas)*

Prayers/Salutations	प्रार्थन
These prayers may be chanted by the priest, the principals as well as Hindus in the audience familiar with these salutations. 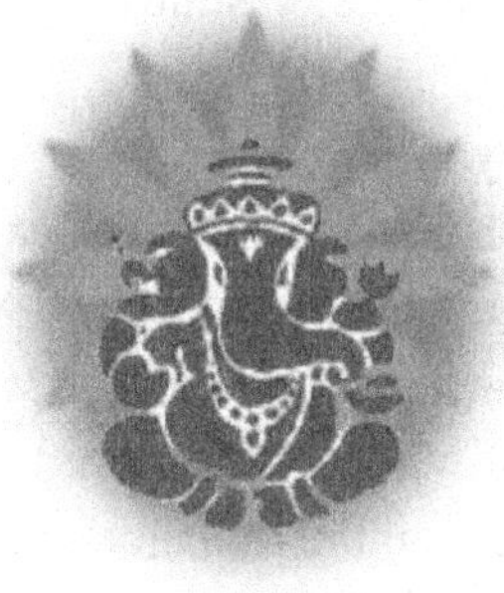	श्रीमन्महागणाधिपतये नमः लक्ष्मी नारायणाभ्याम् नमः उमा महेश्वराभ्याम् नमः श्री सत्यनारायण स्वामिने नमः वाणी हिरण्यगर्भाभ्यं नमः शची पुरंदराभ्यां नमः माता पितृभ्याम् नमः इश्ट देवताभ्यां नमः कुल देवताभ्यां नमः ग्राम देवताभ्यां नमः स्थान देवताभ्यो नमः वास्तु देवताभ्यो नमः आदित्यादि नवग्रहदेवताभ्यो नमः सर्वेभ्यो देवेभ्यो नमः ऐतत्कर्म प्रधान देवताभ्यो नमः अविघ्नमस्तु शुक्लांबरधरं विष्णुं शशिवर्णं चतुर्भुजम् प्रसन्न वदनं ध्यायेत् सर्व विघ्नोप शांतये

prārthana	**Prayers**
śrīmanmahāgaṇādhipatayē nama: *lakṣmī nārāyaṇābhyām nama:* *umā mahēśvarābhyām nama:* *śrī satyanārāyaṇa swāminē nama:* *vāṇī hiraṇyagarbhābhyām nama:* *śachī purandarābhyām nama:*	Salutations to Mahaganapati, Lakshminarayana, Umamaheshwara, Satyanarayana, Vanihiranyagrbha, Shachipurandara.
mātā pitṛbhyām nama: *iṣta dēvatābhyām nama:* *kula dēvatābhyām nama:* *grāma dēvatābhyām nama:* *sthāna dēvatābhyō nama:* *vāstu dēvatābhyō nama:*	Salutations to the mothers and fathers, my chosen godhead, family deity, deity presiding over this town, deity presiding over this place, deity presiding over this building.
ādityādi navagrahadēvatābhyō nama: *sarvēbhyō dēvēbhyō nama:* *ētatkarma pradhāna dēvatābhyō nama:* *avighnamastu*	Salutations to the nine planets, salutations to all godheads, salutation to the godhead presiding over this ceremony. May there be no obstacles.
śuklāmbaradharam viṣṇum *śaśivarṇam caturbhujam* *prasanna vadanam dhyāyēt* *sarva vighnōpa śāntayē*	I meditate on Vishnu who is clothed in white, the color of the moon, four-armed and smiling, to lessen all obstacles.

Sankalpam

The father of the bride, repeating after the priest, declares his intention publicly thus:

This is a declaration of the time and place specified for the rite, here assumed to take place in North America.

संकल्पं

शुभे शोभने मुहूर्ते आद्य ब्रह्मणः द्वितीय परार्धे श्री श्वेत वराह कल्पे वैवस्वत मन्वन्तरे कलियुगे प्रथमे पादे क्रौन्च द्वीपे अमेरिका वर्षे उत्तर अमेरिका खंडे व्यवहारिके चांद्रमानेनस्य षष्टि संवत्सराणां मध्ये ----------- संवत्सरे, ------------- आयने, --- ------- ऋतौ,-------------- मासे, -------------- पक्षे, ---------- -- तिथौ, ----------- नक्षत्रें, ---- -------वासर युक्तायाम्, ऐवं गुण विशेषण विशिष्टायाम् अस्याम् शुभ तिथौ, ------- ----------- नामधेयः अहं मम धर्म पत्नि ---------- देवी सहित मम पुत्री चिरन्जीवि सौभाग्यवति -------- देवी नाम्नि शुभ विवाह महोत्सवांगाय -------- - गोत्रोद्भवस्य -----------नामधेयः अस्याम् वराणाम् तथा तस्य कुटुंबानाम् कन्यादान समये सुस्वागत तथा वर पूजां करिष्ये

Sankalpam	Declaration of Space/Time
śubhē śōbhana muhūrtē, ādya brahmaṇa:, dvitīya parārdhē, śrī śvēta varāha kalpē, vaivasvata manvantarē, kaliyugē, prathama pādē, kraunca dvīpē, amerikā varṣē, uttara amerikā khanḍē, vyavahārikē, cāndramānēnasya ṣaṣṭhi samvatsarāṇām madhyē, --------------- samvatsarē, -------------------āyanē, ----------- ṛtau,------------ māsē, ------------ pakṣē, ----------- tiṭhau, ----------- nakṣatrē,-----------vāsara yuktāyām, ēvam guṇa viśēṣaṇa viśṣṭhāyām asyām shubha tiṭhau, ----------------- nāmadhēya: aham mama dharma patnī --------- dēvī sahita mama putrī chiranjīvi saubhāgyavati ---------- ------- dēvī nāmni shubha vivāha mahōtsavāngāya ------------------------ gōtrōdbhavasya ---------------------------- nāmadhēya: asyām varāṇām taṭhā tasya kutumbānām kanyādāna samayē susvāgata taṭhā vara pūjām kariṣyē.	At this most auspicious time in the earliest part of the second half of Brahma's term of Vaivasvata in the White Boar's millennium, in the first segment of Kali Yuga, in North America, in the general region of America, in the island of Krauncha (Heron), specifying, under normal practice, among the sixty Chaandramana years beginning with Prabhava, ------------ year, -------------- solstice, ------------ season, ------------- month, -------------- position of the moon, ------------- the lunar day, ---------------star, ---------------- day, on such superior time and particular day, I -----------------along with --------------my wife-in-dharma, declare my intention to welcome this bridegroom -------------------, born in ------------ gotra, and his family, in order to offer Vara Puja in connection with the auspicious wedding of my daughter Chiranjeevi Saubhaagyavati ---------------------------------- Devi.

Vara Puja

Short Version

This dialogue may take place at the Milni stage if an elaborate version will be used at the mantap. Otherwise this version is all that is necessary and will suffice for use at the mantap.

The dialogue begins with a greeting from the bride's father and continues as shown with a final mandate from the priest.

वर पूजा

कर्तृः ओं साधु भवान् आस्ताम्
वरः वृतोस्मि
– ओं साधुं अहमासे
कर्तृः अर्चयिष्यामो भवंतं
वरः अर्चय

पुरोहितः

गृहस्थाश्रम सिध्यर्थं चतुर्विध
फल पुरुषार्थ सिध्यर्थं
शुभ विवाह विधिं
यथा विहितं कर्म कुरु

वरः यथा ज्नानं करवाणि

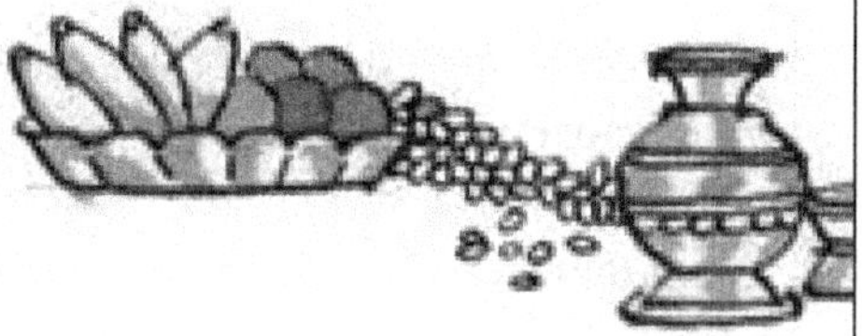

Vara Puja	**Vara Puja (Short Version)**
kartṛ: *ōm sādhu bhavān āstām*	**The initiator** (bride's father): May you receive this honor from us.
vara: *vṛtōsmi - ōm sādhum ahamāsē*	**Bridegroom**: I am satisfied. I am honored.
kartṛ: *arcayiśyāmō bhavantam*	**Bride's father**: We worship your virtues.
vara: *arcaya*	**Bridegroom**: I am honored.
purōhita *gṛhasṭhāśrama sidhyarṭham* *caturvidha phala puruṣhārṭha sidhyarṭham* *śubha vivāha vidhim* *yaṭhā vihitam karma kuru*	**Priest** In order to attain the next stage of Householder and in order to attain the fruits of the four aspects of life, prepare yourself to perform the auspicious wedding rites according to prescribed shastras.
vara: *yaṭhā jnānam karavāṇi*	**Groom**: I shall do so to the best of my knowledge (ability).
	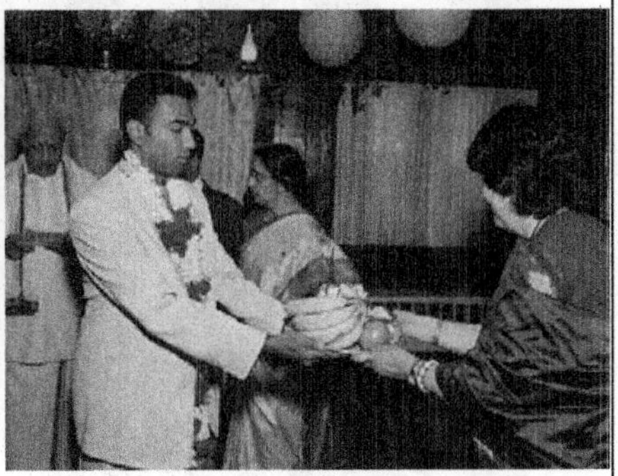

Vara Puja	दाता
(Longer Version) In this version the dialogue is longer and covers the *shodashopacharas* i.e. the steps used in performing a puja to a deity except that in this case the object of the worship (the groom) responds in appreciation of the puja rendered to him. Note that the step in which the bride's mother offers an arati may be omitted if she has already taken this step at the Milni. 	मम कुमार्या: उद्वाहार्थं आगतं श्री लक्श्मीनारायण स्वरूप वर तुभ्यं गंध पुष्प अक्षताभि: पूजयिष्ये वर: अस्तु दाता श्री लक्ष्मीनारायण स्वरूपस्य वरस्ट इदमासनं वर: सुखासनं दाता श्री लक्ष्मीनारायणं भवत्सु आवाहयिष्ये वर: आवाहय दाता भागश: अमीवो गंधा: वर: सुगंधा: दाता इमानिवपुष्पाणि पुष्प मालिकाम् वर: सुपुष्पाणि दाता अयंवो धूप: वर: सुधूप: दाता अयंवो दीप: वर: सुदीप: कन्या माता श्री लक्श्मीनारायण स्वरूप वर इदं नीराजनं वर: सुनीराजनं

dātā	**Giver**
mama kumāryāha udvāhārṭham āgatam śrī lakṣmīnārāyaṇa svarūpāya varam tubhyam gandha puṣpa akṣhatābhi: pūjayiśyē	I offer sandal paste, flowers, akshata in worshipping you, the very embodiment of Lakshminarayana, in the course of my daughter's wedding rituals.
***vara**: astu*	**Groom**: May it be so.
dātā	**Giver**
śrī lakṣmīnārāyaṇa svarūpasya idamāsanam	This is the seat for you in the form of Lakshminarayana.
***vara**: sukhāsanam*	**Groom**: A comfortable seat.
dātā	**Giver**
śrī lakṣmīnārāyaṇam bhavatsu āvāhayiṣyē	I invoke you in the form of Lakshminarayana.
***vara**: āvāhaya*	**Groom**: Please do.
dātā	**Giver**
bhāgasha: amīvō gandhā:	As part (of the worship) here is sandal paste.
***vara**: sugandhā:*	**Groom**:Good fragrance.
dātā	**Giver**
imānivapuṣpāṇi puṣpa mālikām	Here is the garland of flowers.
***vara:** supuṣpāṇi*	**Groom**:Good flowers.
***dātā:** ayamvō dhūpa:*	**Giver**: Here is fragrance.
***vara**: sudhūpa:*	**Groom**: Good fragrance.
***dātā**: ayamvō dīpa:*	**Giver**: Here is the light.
***vara**: sudīpa:*	**Groom**: Good light.
kanyā mātā	**Bride's mother**
śrī lakṣmīnārāyaṇa svarūpāya vara idaṃ nīrājana	Here is arati to the groom in the form of Lakshminarayana.
***vara**: sunīrājanam*	**Groom**: Good arati.

The Vara Puja is complete with the final offerings as shown here and the stage is now set for the arrival of the bride.

The coordinator signals the person in charge of conducting the bride to the hall, traditionally her maternal uncle, close to the moment when the bride's mother conducts the arati (in the elaborate version). As stated earlier if the brief version is chosen then the cue for the coordinator is when the brief Vara Puja dialogue begins on stage.

दाता

गंध पुष्प धूप दीप सकलाराधनैः स्वर्चितं

वर

अस्तु

dātā *gandha puṣpa dhūpa dīpa sakalāradhanai: svarcitam* **Vara** astu 	**Giver** We worship you elaborately with sandal, flowers, fragrance and lamp. **Groom** May it be so. 

Antarpat*

As the bridal procession approaches the mantap, the bride, escorted by her maternal uncle or other relative, is helped by her maid of honor while the other bridesmaids take previously planned positions. The bride stands in front of the cloth shield (antarpat), facing the groom. The ceremony begins with the groom reciting the mantras shown here or repeating after the priest.

Remove the curtain at the end of this chant. (* Note: If the family practice is to omit Antarpat, then the garlanding ceremony may proceed in the way described here by omitting all actions pertaining to the curtain)

अंतर्पट

आनः प्रजां जनयतु प्रजापतिः
आजरसाय समनक्त्वर्यमा
अभ्रातृघ्नीं वरुणा
अपतिघ्नीं बृहस्पते
इन्द्रा पुत्रघ्नीं
लक्ष्म्यंतामस्यै सवितस्सुव
अघोर चक्षुर् अपतिघ्न्येधि
शिवा पतिभ्यस्सुमना स्सु वर्चाः
वीरसूर् देवकामा स्योना शंनो भव
द्विपदे शंचतुष्पदे

Antarpat	**Antarpat**
āna: prajām janayatu prajāpati: ājarasāya samanaktvaryamā abhrātr̥ghnīm varuṇā apatighnīm br̥haspatē indrā putraghnīm lakṣmyamtāmasyai savitassuva *aghōra cakṣur apatighnyēdhi shivā patibhyassumanā ssu varchā: vīrasūr dēvakāmā syōnā śamnō bhava dvipadē shamcatuśpadē* 	May Prajaapati bless her with children, May Aryama bless her jewelry, May Varuna and Brhaspati protect her husband and his brothers, May Indra protect her children, May Savitr grant her wealth. O Bride, may your peaceful demeanor and compassion provide peace in my family. May you bear brave children and bring happiness to both humans and animals. 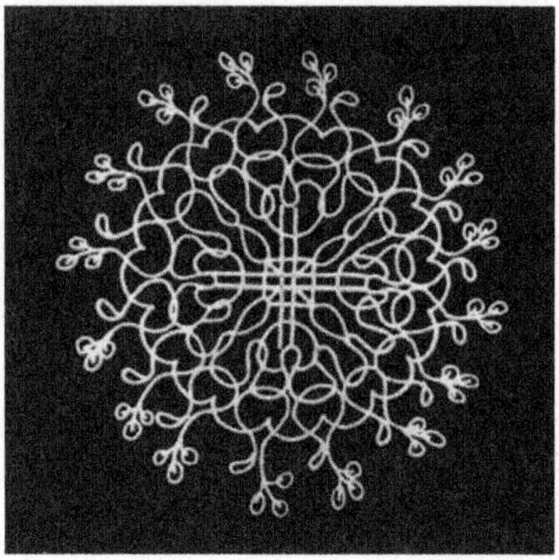

Jayamala

The couple face each other.
The maid of honor hands a garland to the bride while at the same time the best man assists the groom to take off the garland that is now on his neck.

The bride garlands the groom who in turn takes the garland from the hand of the best man and garlands the bride. With both garlanded now they face the audience with the bride standing to the right of the groom.

I have taken the liberty of using सोहम् अस्मि instead of amoahamasmi because in context सोहम् appears to be more appropriate and in tune with सा त्वं. (Atharva Veda 14.2.71)

जयमाल

संज्नानं विज्नानं जानदभि जानत्
संकल्पमानं प्रकल्पमानं उपकल्पमानं
उपक्लुप्तं क्ल्प्तं
श्रेयोवसीय आयत्संभूतं भूतम्
चित्रकेतुः प्रभानाथ्संभान्
ज्योतिष्मागंस्तेजस्वानातपग्
स्तपन्नभितपन्
रोचनो रोचमान श्शोभन
श्शोभन कल्याणः

सुमंगलीरियं वधूरिमां समेत पश्यत
सोहम् अस्मि सा त्वं सामाहमस्म्य
ऋक्त्वं द्यौरहं पृथिवी त्वं ताविह
संभवाव प्रजामा जनयावहै

samjnānam vijnānam prajnānam jānadabhi jānat, sankalpamānam prakalpamānam upakalpamānam upakluptam kluptam śrēyōvasīya āyatsambhūtam bhūtam chitrakētu: prabhānāṭh sambhānām jyōtiṣmāgamstējasvānātapag stapannabhitapan rōcanō rōcamāna śśōbhana śśōbhamāna kalyāṇa:	This bride possesses superior intelligence to bring harmony between the families; decisive, honorable, desirous of and ready to make a home. She arrives truly beautiful, distinguished as a bright shining light, gleaming with luster, charming, pleasing and lovely Hail this bride.
sumangalīriyam vadhūrimām samēta paśyata	Let all look at this bride who is auspicious.
sōham asmi sā tvam sāmāhamasmya ṛktvam dyauraham pṛṭhivī tvam tāviha sambhavāva prajāmā janayāvahē 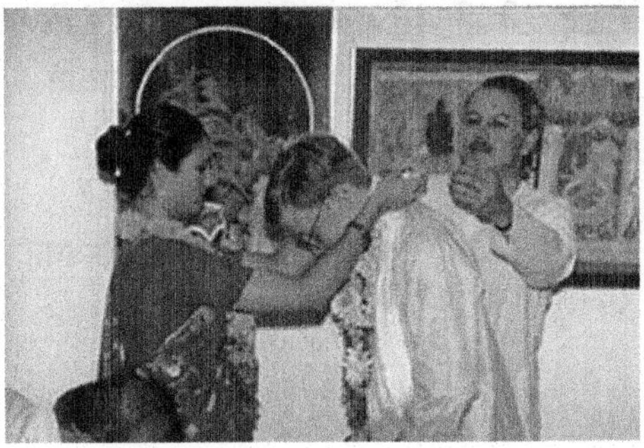	I am He, you are She I am Song, you are Verse I am Heaven, you are Earth. Let us both dwell together here, parents of future children

Hasta Milap

Subsequent to garlanding and as the bride and groom turn to face the audience, the bride's father steps up and places the right hand of his daughter in the right hand of the groom.
The groom is instructed to chant the mantra, I hold your hand …

Priest: Pravara Recital

This step is a formal public announcement of the of the names of the bridegroom and the bride in front of the assembled. They are introduced formally declaring their lineage beginning with great grandfather and proceeding with grandfather and father. This serves as an opportunity to remember the ancestors in both families on this auspicious occasion. Normally the practice is to repeat the Pravara recital three times. But it may be done only once.

Father, Giver of the bride, recites the last verse.

हस्तमिलाप्

गृभ्णामि ते सुप्रजास्त्वाय हस्तंमया
पत्या जरदश्टिर्यथासः
भगोअर्यमा सविता
पुरंधिर्मह्यंत्वादुर्गार्ह पत्याय देवाः

प्रवर

त्रया ऋषयः (पंचार्षयः , सप्तार्षयः)
प्रवरान्विताय .... गोत्रोत्पन्नयां
......................प्रपौत्रायां, ... पौत्रायां,
श्रीमान् .... तथा श्रीमति
सौभाग्यवति .... देवि पुत्रायां,
श्रीधर रूपिणी चिरंजीवि .... नाम्ने
वराय,
त्रया ऋषयः (पंचार्षयः) प्रवरोपेतां
.......................गोत्रोत्पन्नां ....प्रपौत्रीं,
........................पौत्रीं, श्रीमान् ....
तथा श्रीमति सौभाग्यवति .... देवि पुत्रीं,
श्री रूपिणी, चिरंजीवि सौभाग्यवति
.... नाम्नी कन्यां,

प्रजापति दैवत्यां प्रजोत्पादनार्तं तुभ्यमहं
संप्रददे नमम

gr̥bhṇāmi tē suprajāstvāya hastam mayā patyā jaradaśṭir yaṭhāasa: bhagōaryamā savitā purandhirmahyamtvādurgārha patyāya dēvā:	O bride, I shall hold your hand in order to live long with you and our progeny through the grace of Aryama, Savitr and Indra who have granted us the status of householders.
trayā r̥ṣaya: (pancārṣaya: , saptārṣaya:) pravarānvitāya .... gōtrōtpannayām ....prapautrāyām, ...pautrāyām, śrīmān .... taṭhā śrīmati saubhāgyavati .... dēvi putrāyām, ciranjīvi .... nāmnē varāya,*	Spiritual descendent of three sages (five or seven sages*), born in the ------------ gotra, the great grandson of -------------, -------------, grandson of ----------------, son of Mr.----------------- and Mrs. Saubhagyavati -------------------------, Chiranjivi ------------------------------, the bridegroom
trayā r̥ṣaya: pravarōpētam .... gōtrōtpannām ....prapautrīm, ...pautrīm, śrīmān .... taṭhā śrīmati saubhāgyavati .... dēvi putrīm, ciranjīvi saubhāgyavati .... nāmnī kanyām,	Spiritual descendent of three sages (five or seven sages), born in the ------------- gotra, great granddaughter of ----------------------, granddaughter of --------------, and daughter of Mr. ----------------- and Mrs. Saubhagyavati --------------------, Chiranjivi Saubhagyavati -----------, the bride,
prajāpati daivatyām prajōtpādanārṭham tubhyamaham sampradadē namama	And in order to propitiate Brahma, the lord of progeny, and in order to continue my lineage, I bestow this young woman on you without any reservation. Please accept her. She is all yours.
	* Some gotras refer to 5 or 7 sages.

Kanyadanam

This important ritual begins with a call to the audience to bless this moment to be auspicious. This and similar requests throughout the ceremony not only engage the audience but serve notice that the assembled are witness to an important commitment being made at the mantap. Everyone present is requested to respond with "tathastu" at the end of each phrase.

With this set of permissions granted the Kanyadanam ceremony may now begin.

कन्यादानम्

अनुज्ने

अयं मुहूर्तस्सुमुहूर्तोस्त्विति
भवान्तो महांतो अनुगृह्णंतु

कर्तव्ये अस्मिन् शुभ विवाह कर्मणि
भवान्तो महांतो अधिब्रुवंतु

ओं पुण्याहं भवंतो अधिब्रुवंतु
ओं ऋध्धिं भवंतो अधिब्रुवंतु
ओं स्वस्ति भवंतो अधिब्रुवंतु

कन्यां कनक संपन्नां कनकाभरणैर्युतां
दास्यामि विष्णवे तुभ्यं ब्रह्म लोक जिगीषया
कन्ये ममाग्रतो भूयात् कन्येमे देविपार्श्वयोः
कन्येमे सर्वतो भूयात् त्वद्दानान्मोक्षमाप्नुयां

विश्वंभराः सर्वभूताः साक्षिण्यः सर्वदेवताः
इमां कन्यां प्रदास्यामि पितृणां तारणायच
कन्यां सालंकृत्वा साध्वीं सुशीलाय सुधीमते
प्रयतोहं प्रदास्यामि धर्म काम्यार्थ सिद्धये

anujne	**Permission**
ayam muhūrtassumuhūrtōstviti *bhavāntō mahāntō anugr̥ṇhantu*	May you, the great assembled, grant this present time to be auspicious.
kartavyē asmin śubha vivāha karmaṇi *bhavāntō mahāntō adhibruvantu*	May you, the great assembled, express that this wedding task be auspicious.
om puṇyāham bhavantō adhibruvantu *om r̥dhdhim bhavantō adhibruvantu* *om svasti bhavantō adhibruvantu*	May you express this day to be auspicious. May you express this to be successful. May you express your blessings.
kanyādānam	**Gift of the bride**
kanyām kanaka sampannām *kanakābharaṇairyutām* *dāsyāmi viṣṇuvē tubhyam brahma lōka* *jigīśayā kanyē mamāgratō bhūyāt* *kanyēmē dēvipārśvayō:* *kanyēmē sarvatō bhūyāt tvaddānān* *mōkṣamāpnuyām*	May I offer to you, the embodiment of Vishnu, this, my daughter, foremost among all young women, by my side, covered with golden ornaments, so that I may obtain salvation in Brahmaloka.
viśvambharā: sarvabhūtā: sākṣiṇya: *sarvadēvatā: imām kanyṇām* *pradāsyāmi pitr̥ṇām tāraṇāyaca* *kanyām sālamkr̥tvā sādhvīm suśīlāya* *sudhīmatē prayatōham pradāsyāmi* *dharma kāmyārṭha siddhayē*	With all gods and other beings as witness, in order to liberate my ancestors and to accomplish dharma, artha and kama, I give away this gift, my daughter who is virtuous, intelligent and beautifully adorned.

Upon these statements of purpose the priest arranges the hands of the principals as follows:

On the outstretched palms of the bride, place the outstretched palms of the groom and on the palms of the groom, place those of the bride's father. On the the topmost palms (bride's father's) place a coconut smeared with kumkum and haldi.
The three stand such that the assembly gets a clear view. The bride's mother is now positioned behind the three and is facing the audience squarely.

As the priest (or the bride's father) chants the following mantras the bride's mother pours water over the coconut in a thin stream and the audience is requested once again to say "tathastu" (it shall be so) at the end of each phrase.

A child needs to be positioned to hold a bowl below to collect the water.
The water should continue to be poured in a thin stream until all the phrases are chanted.

During this sequence the mangalsutra is taken around to be blessed by the elders present.

श्रीरूपिणीं इमां कन्यां श्रीधर रूपिणे
तुभ्यं इत्युक्त्वा उदक पूर्वांतां
कायेनवाचामनसा ददाम्यस्मै

कन्या तारयतु
पुण्यं वर्धतां
सौमनस्यमस्तु
अक्षतं चरिष्टं चास्तु
दीर्घमायुः श्रेयः शान्तिः पुश्टिः तुश्टिःचास्तु
यछ्रेयस्तदस्तु
यत् पापं तत्प्रतिहतस्तु
पुण्याहं भवंतो ब्रुवन्तु
स्वस्ति भवंतो ब्रुवंतु
ऋध्धिं भवंतो ब्रुवंतु
श्रीरस्त्विति भवंतो ब्रुवंतु

śrīrūpiṇīm imām kanyām śrīdhara
rūpiṇē tubhyam ityuktva udaka
pūrvāntām kāyēnavācāa manasā
dadāmyasmai

kanyā tārayatu
puṇyam vardhatām
saumanasyamastu
akśatam cāriśtam cāstu
dīrghamāyu: śrēya:
śānti: puṣṭi: tuṣṭi:cāstu
yacchrēyastadastu
yat pāpam tatpratihatastu
puṇyāham bhavantō bruvantu
svasti bhavantō bruvantu
ṛdhdhim bhavantō bruvantu
śrīrastviti bhavantō bruvantu

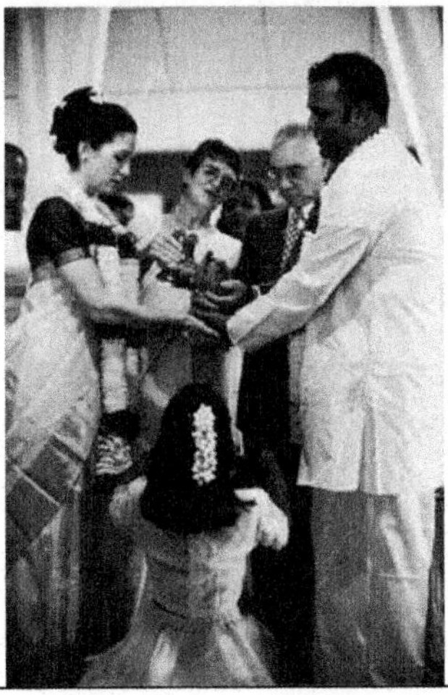

With this in my mind, with these words and with this act before the ceremonial water is poured, May I offer you, who are in the form of Vishnu, this, my daughter in the form of Lakshmi.

May my daughter gain protection
May holiness prosper
May there be joy
May she be whole
May she live long, prosper, be at peace, well nourished and content
May prosperity prevail
May any ills be struck down
May you grant this day to be a happy one
May you bless her wellbeing
May you grant her abundance
May you grant her respect and status

Mangalyadharanam

मांगल्य धारणं/Māngalyadhāraṇam

Among the various traditions practiced in wedding ceremonies, the South Indian tradition considers the tying of the mangalasutra necklace by the groom around the bride's neck as the point at which the couple is declared married. In the old days, in India, unuttered sighs of relief could be seen on the faces of the bride's family upon completion of this step because the "responsibility" to care for the young woman was now officially transferred from the parents of the bride to the young man.

Ritualistic requirements in this ceremony include the following:

1. The māngalya or mangalasutra necklace is taken around, prior to the ceremony, to be blessed by the elders in both families. The designated person upon cue (as Kanyādānam water is being poured) from the coordinator takes the plate on which the necklace rests on a colorful silk cloth and shows it to the elder as if it is being offered to the person. The elder then simply places both of his/her hands, palms down, on the plate as if to cover it. That gesture is blessing and is considered imperative.
2. The groom worships the māngalya godhead because the belief is that a goddess protects it.
3. Approval of the assembled is sought.
4. The bride is blessed by the priest.
5. The groom ties the necklace, as he prays for his longevity, assisted by his sister who positions herself behind the bride to make sure the knot (or the clasp) is tied securely. Some traditions require her and the groom's mother to tie a second and third knot.

Generally the practice has been to increase the volume of music (a particularly loud drum roll in South Indian tradition) to mark the climactic moment. Upon completion of the tying, the bride's father once again confirms the offer of the bride and stipulates and extracts a promise that the groom lead a virtuous life and not transgress the boundaries of dharma, artha and kama. The groom gives his word and thus he is now a husband and she is his wife.

Mangalyadharanam	मांगल्य धारणम्
The groom first does ācamanam, that is, he sips water three times after praying to Acyuta, Ananta and Gōvinda respectively.	वरः आचमनम्
The māngalya, blessed by elders, is brought to the priest.	मांगल्य देवताभ्यो नमः; ध्यायामि, आवाहयामि आसनं समर्पयामि नानाविध परिमळ पत्र पुष्प फलानि समर्पयामि
The groom offers worship to the māngalya:	अनया पूजया भगवती श्री मांगल्य महालक्ष्मी देवी सुप्रीता सुप्रसन्ना वरदा भवतु ध्रुवंते राजा वरुणो ध्रुवं देवो बृहस्पतिः ध्रुवंत इंद्रश्चाग्निश्च राष्ट्रं धारयतां ध्रुवं ध्रुवं
Anujna	अनुज्न
The priest seeks permission of the assembly to grant the moment to be auspicious.	मांगल्य धारण मुहूर्त स्सुमुहूर्तोस्त्विति भवान्तो महांतो अनुगृह्णंतु सुमुहूर्तोस्तु
The priest puts akṣhata on the bride's head as he blesses her just prior to the tying of the mangalasūtra.	दीर्घ सुमंगली भव आयुरारोग्य ऐश्वर्य संपत् समृद्धा भव गृहस्थाश्रमे शुभनि वर्धताम्

Māngalyadhāraṇam	**Tying the Mangalya**
māngalya dēvatābhyō nama dhyāyāmi, āvāhayāmi āsanam samarpayāmi nānāvidha parimaḷa patra puṣpa phalāni samarpayāmi	Salutations to the goddess of this mangalya. I meditate upon her, invoke her, offer her a seat and a variety of perfumes, leaves, flowers and fruits.
anayā pūjayā bhagavatī śrī māngalya mahālakṣmī dēvī suprītā suprasannā varadā bhavatu	May you goddess Mahalakshmi of this mangalya be pleased with this puja.
dhruvantē rājā varuṇō dhruvam dēvō bṛhaspati: dhruvanta indraścāgniśca rāṣtram dhārayatām dhruvam dhruvam	May your realm be as firm as that of King Varuna, gods Brhaspati, Indra and Agni.
Anujna	**Permission**
māngalya dhāraṇa muhūrtassumuhōrtōstviti bhavāntō mahāntō anugṛṇhantu sumuhūrtōstu	May all the great assembled grant this moment of tying the mangalya to be especially auspicious. May this be a specially auspicious moment.
dīrgha sumangalī bhava āyurārōgya aiśvarya sampat samṛddhā bhava gṛhasṭhāśramē śubhāni vardhatām	May your husband live long. May you both live long and may your life be filled with health, wealth and be plentiful. May your life as a householder prosper well.

The Tying of the Māngalya	धारणम्
The groom picks up the necklace and chants.	मांगल्यं तंतुनानेन मम जीवन हेतुना कंठे बध्नामि सुभगे त्वं जीव शरदश्शतम्
The groom ties the sutra around the bride's neck. Some traditions require a second or third knot tied by the mother and/or sister of the groom.	मंगळं भगवान् विष्णुः मंगळं मधुसूदनः मंगळं पुंडरीकाक्षो मंगळं गरुडध्वजः
Priest sprinkles flowers on the bride.	वधु/पुष्पं दाताः
Bride's father puts flower petals on her head and chants. Bride's father charges the groom asking him not to transgress the boundaries of dharma, artha and kama.	गौरीं कन्यां इमां विप्र यथा शक्ति विभूषितां ...... गोत्रोद्भवस्य ...... तुभ्यं दत्तां विप्र समाश्रय कन्ये ममाग्रतो भूयाः कन्येमे देवि पार्श्वयोः कन्येमे षष्ठतो भूयाः त्वद्दानात् मोक्षमाप्नुयां मम वंश कुले जाता पालिका वत्स राष्टकं तुभ्यं विप्र मया दत्त पुत्र पौत्र प्रवर्धिनीं धर्मेचार्थेच कामेच नाति चरितव्या त्वमेयं
The groom responds affirmatively. Then the bride is instructed to move to his left.	वरः नाति चरामि

Dhāraṇam	**The Tying of the Māngalya**
māngalyam tantunānēna mama jīvana hētunā kanṭē badhnāmi subhagē tvam jīva śaradaśśatam	The yellow thread here (mangalasutra) will enhance my longevity. I tie it on your neck as I pray that you live happily for a hundred years.
mangaḷam bhagavān viṣṇu: mangaḷam madhusūdana: mangaḷam pundarīkākṣō mangaḷam garudadhvaja:	May it please the gods, the various avatars of Vishnu; Madhusudana, Pundarikaksha and Krishna.
vadhu/puṣpam/dātā	
dātā	Giver (of the bride):
gaurīm kanyām imām vipra yaṭhā śakti vibhūṣitām .... gōtrōdbhavasya ...... tubham dattām vipra samāśraya kanyē mamāgratō bhūyā: kanyēmē dēvi pārśvayō: kanyēmē ṣaṣṭhatō bhūyā: tvaddānān mōkṣamāpnuyām mama vamsha kulē jātā pālikā vatsa rāṣtakam tubhyam vipra mayā datta putra pautra pravardhinīm dharmēcārṭhēca kāmēca nāti caritavyā tvamēyam	So that I may get liberation and so that you may have children and grandchildren, I offer you, the gentleman born in ....gotra, this foremost among young women, my daughter, born and brought up in my family, standing near me here prominently, adorned to the best of our ability. Provide support and comfort to her and never transgress the boundaries of dharma, artha and kaama.
vara: nāti carāmi	Bridegroom: I shall not transgress.

Blessing the Bride

The priest chants a charge to the bride and blesses her, reciting the same blessing used by Queen Kunti.

फुरोहित

यथेंद्राणि महेंद्रस्य
स्वाहाचैव विभावसोः
रोहिणीच यथा सोमे
दमयंती यथा नळे
यथा वैवस्वते भद्रा
वसिष्ठे चापि अरुंधती
यथा नारायणी लक्ष्मी
तथा त्वं भवभर्तारि

दीर्घ सुमंगली भव

Purōhita	**Priest's blessing**
yathēndrāṇi mahēndrasya *svāhāchaiva vibhāvasō:* *rōhiṇīca yathā sōmē* *damayantī yathā naḷē* *yathā vaivasvatō bhadrā* *vasiṣṭē cāpi arundhatī* *yathā nārāyanī lakṣmī* *tathā tvam bhavabhartāri*	As Shachi to Indra, as Swaha to Agni, as Rohini to Chandra, as Damayanti to Nala, as Bhadra to Vivasvat, as Arundhati to Vasishta, as Lakshmi to Vishnu, may you be to your husband.

Pradhana Homa

Primary Fire Ritual

The priest begins this ceremony with a prayer to Agni by touching the front of the kunda with both palms and bringing the palms to the eyes to show reverence to the fire god. The most appropriate shloka chosen for this beginning prayer is the very first shloka in the very first hymn in the very first book of the Rig Veda. The beauty and relevance of this stanza is that it hails Agni and acknowledges him as the priest.

Next using the ceremonial spoon (uddharana) the priest sprinkles water as the following four appeals are made by reciting each phrase successively along with the sprinkling as described below:

First sprinkle on the right side of the agnikunda going from lower side to the upper side, then on the lower side going from right to left and the third from lower side to upper side on the left of the agnikunda. The final sprinkling is clockwise all around.

प्रधान होम

ओं अग्निमीळे पुरोहितं
यज्नस्य देवमृत्विजं
होतारं रत्न धातमं

परिषेचनम्
ओं अदितेनुमन्यस्वा
ओं अनुमतेनुमन्यस्वा
ओं सरस्वतेनुमन्वस्वा
ओं देव सवितः प्रसुव

Pradhānahoma	**Primary Fire Ritual**
ōm agnimīḻē purōhitam yajnasya dēvamṛtvijam hōtāram ratna dhātamam	Om Praise be to Agni, the domestic priest, God, minister of ritual, the invoker and lavisher of wealth upon his devotees *Rig Veda (1.1.1)*

pariṣēcanam	Ceremonial sprinkling
ōm aditēnumanyasvā ōm anumatēnumanyasvā ōm saraswatēnumanvasvā ōm dēva savita: prasuva	Om, O Aditi, appear on this side here Om, O Anumati, appear on this side here. Om, O Saraswati, appear on this side here. Om, O Sun God, appear completely here.

The Homas

An assistant must now be ready with the samagris (offerings of ghee, rice, incense) for use by the couple. First the priest instructs the groom to declare his intention to perform the homas.

प्रतिगृहीतायां अस्यां वध्वां
भार्यात्व सिध्धयै गृह्यात्व सिध्धयेच
विवाह होमं करिष्ये
तदंग योजक नामाग्नि प्रतिष्ठापने विनियोगः

The particular aspect of Agni invoked is Yojaka who, in this context, means Preparer, i.e. Agni whose grace is sought to prepare for the new status and for a secure union.

ओं अग्नये स्वाहा– अग्नय इदं नमम
ओं सोमाय स्वाहा – सोमाय इदं नमम
ओं भूर्भुवस्व स्वाहा – प्रजापतय इदं नमम

The groom chants all mantras or repeats after the priest. He offers oblations with the samagris handed over to him by the assistant.

ओं सोमाय स्वाहा – सोमाय इदं नमम
ओं अग्नये स्वाहा– अग्नय इदं नमम
ओं भूर्भुवस्व स्वाहा – प्रजापतय इदं नमम

Note: These first offerings are made to the former spiritual husbands (guardians Soma, Gandharva and Agni) of the bride and thus acknowledges them at the very beginning of this yajna (sacrifice).

सोमाय जनिविदे स्वाहा
सोमाय जनिविद इदं नमम
गंधर्वाय जनिविदे स्वाहा
गंधर्वाय जनिविद इदं नमम
अग्नये जनिविदे स्वाहा
अग्नये जनिविद इदं नमम

pratigṛhītāyām asyām vadhvām bhāryātva siddhdhayē gṛhyātva siddhayēca vivāha hōmam kariṣyē tadanga yōjaka nāmāgni pratiṣṭhāpanē viniyōga:	So that I may receive this bride, to gain her as a wife and to gain the status of a householder, I shall perform the wedding sacrificial rites. And as a part of the ceremony, I shall take the task of establishing Agni of the name Yojaka.
ōm agnayē svāhā- agnaya idam namama *ōm sōmāya svāhā - somayē idam namama* *ōm bhūrbhuvsva svāhā - prajāpataya idam namama*	Towards the north of the Agnikunda: Hail to Agni: this is yours, not mine Hail to Soma: this is yours, not mine Hail to the three worlds: this is that of the divinity of procreation, not mine.
ōm sōmāya svāhā - sōmayē idam namama *ōm agnayē svāhā- agnaya idam namama* *ōm bhūrbhuvasva svāhā - prajāpataya idam namama*	Towards the south of the Agnikunda: Hail to Soma: this is yours, not mine Hail to Agni: this is yours, not mine Hail to the three worlds: this is that of the divinity of procreation, not mine.
sōmāya janividē svāhā sōmāya janivida idam namama *gandharvāya janividē svāhā gandharvāya janivida idam namama* *agnayē janividē svāhā agnayē janivida idam namama*	This oblation is to Soma who knew this bride as a wife. This belongs to that knowledge, not mine. This oblation is to the Gandharva who knew this bride as a wife. This belongs to that knowledge, not mine. This oblation is to Agni who knew this bride as a wife. This belongs to that knowledge, not mine.

कन्यला पितृभ्यो यती पतिलोकमाव
दीक्षामदास्थ स्वाहा
वध्वै सूर्याय इदं नमम

प्रेतोमुंचाति नामुतस्सुबध्धाममुतस्करत्
यथेयमिन्द्र मीढ्व स्सुपुत्रा सुभगासति स्वाहा
इंद्राय मीढुष इदं नमम

इमांत्वं इन्द्रमीड्व स्सुपुत्राग्ं सुभगां कृणु
दशास्यां पुत्रानाधेहि पतिमेकादशं कृधिस्वाहा
इंद्राय मीढुष इदं नमम

अग्निरैतु प्रथमो देवतानाग्ं सोस्यै प्रजां
मुंचतु मृत्युपाशात्
तदयग्ं राजा वरुणोनुमन्यतां
यथेयग्ग्ं स्त्री पौत्रमघं नरोदात्स्वाहा
अग्नी वरुणाभ्यामिदं नमम

इमामग्नि स्त्रायतां गार्हपत्यः प्रजामस्यै
नयतु दीर्घमायुः अशून्योपस्था जीवतामस्तु
माता पौत्रमानंदमभि प्रभुध्यतामियं स्वाहा
अग्नये गार्हपत्यायेदं नमम

kanyalā pitṛbhyō yatī patilōkamāva deekṣāmadāstha svāhā vadhvai sūryāya idam namama	This young woman is on her way to her husband's family leaving behind her own. Thus this oblation belongs to Sooryaa in the form of this bride, not to me.
prētōmuncāti nāmutassubaddhāmamutaskarat yathēyamindra mīḍhva ssuputrā subhagāsati svāhā indrāya mīḍhuṣa idam namama	May Indra who blesses the earth with rain grant her a stable and prosperous life with children and prosperity. This therefore is Indra's oblation, not mine.
imāmtvam indramīḍva ssuputrāgm subhagām kṛṇu dashāsyām putrānādhēhi patimēkādaśam kṛdhisvāhā indrāya mīḍhuṣa idam namama	O Indra, bestow on this bride virtuous sons and prosperity. Grant her ten sons and let her husband be the eleventh. This oblation is therefore Indra's, not mine.
agniraitu prathamō dēvatānāgm sōsyai prajām muncatu mṛtyupāśāt tadyagm rājā varuṇōnumanyatām yathēyaggm strī pautramagham narōdātsvāhā agnī varuṇābhyāmidam namama	Let Agni, the first among devatas, be present to protect her children from the noose of death. Let Varuna follow suit. Thus protected, let the bride never weep for her progeny. This therefore is Agni's and Varuna's oblation, not mine.
imāmagni strāyatām gārhapatya: prajāmasyai nayatu dīrghamāyu: ashūnyōpasthā jīvatāmastu mātā pautramānandamabhi prabhudhyatāmiyam svāhā agnayē gārhapatyāyēdam namama	Let the sacrificial fire Gaarhapatya (householder's fire) protect this bride and her children for a long time. Let her live as a mother and awaken to the bliss of progeny. This therefore is Gaarhapatya's oblation, not mine.

मा तेगृहे निशिघोष उत्थादन्यत्र त्वद्रुदत्य
स्संविशंतु मात्वं विकेष्युर आवधिष्ठा जीवपत्नी
पतिलोके विराज पश्यन्ती प्रजागं
सुमन्स्यमानां स्वाहा
वध्वै सूर्यायेदं नमम

द्यौस्ते पृष्ठगं रक्षतु वायुरूरू
अश्विनौच स्तनं धयन्तगं सविताभिरक्षतु
आवाससः परिधानात् बृहस्पतिर् विश्वे देवा
अभि रक्षंतु पश्चात् स्वाहा
द्यौर्वायुरश्च सवितृ बृहस्पतिर्विश्वेभ्यो
देवेभ्य इदं

अप्रजस्तां पौत्रमृत्युं पाप्मानमुतवाघं
शीर्ष्णस्स्रजमिवोन्मुच्य द्विषद्भ्यः प्रति मुंचामि
पाशं स्वाहा वध्वै सूर्यायेदं

mā tēgr̥hē niśighōṣa utthādanyatra tvadrudatya ssamviśantu mātvam vikēṣyura āvadhiṣṭhā jīvapatnī patilōkē virāja paśyantī prajāgm sumansyamānām svāhā vadhvai sūryāyēdam namama	Let there be no sharp cries of distress in your home. May you not weep with disheveled hair and beating on your chest. May you be illustrious in your own home with your husband. May there be no reason not to enjoy seeing your virtuous children. This then is Sooryaa's oblation, in the form of this bride, not mine.
dyaustē pr̥ṣṭhagm rakṣatu vāyurūrō ashvinauca stanam dhayantagam savitābhirakṣatu āvāsasa: paridhānāt br̥haspatir vishvē dēvā abhi rakṣantu paścāt svāhā dyaurvāyurashva savitr̥ br̥haspatirvishvēbhyō dēvēbhya idam	May Heaven protect your back, Vayu your thighs, Ashvins your breasts, the Sun your children, Brhaspati when you are fully dressed in your abode, and Visvedeva hereafter.
aprajastām pautramr̥tyum pāpmānamutavāgham śīrṣṇassrajamivōnmucya dviṣadbhya: prati munchāmi pāsham svāhā vadhvai sūryāyēdam	May you have progeny who live long and suffer no calamity. I shall prevent any attempt by enemies to harm you with a noose by removing it as easily as the garland around your neck. This therefore is the oblation to Suryaa in the form of the bride.

इमं मे वरुणश्रुधीहव मद्याचमृडय
त्वामवस्यु राचके स्वाहा वरुणायेदं नमम

तत्वायामि ब्रह्मणा वंदमानस्तदाशास्ते
यजमानो हविर्भिः अहेडमानो
वरुणेहबोध्युरुशगंस
मान आयुः प्रमोषी स्वाहा
वरुणायेदं नमम

त्वंनो अग्ने वरुणस्य विद्वान् देवस्य हेडो
वयासिसीष्ठाः
यजिष्ठोवह्नितमश्योशुचानो विश्वाद्वेषाग्ंसि
प्रमुमुग्ध्यमत् स्वाहा
अग्नीवरुणाभ्यामिदं नमम

सत्वन्नो अग्ने अवमो भवोती नेदिष्ठो
अस्या उषसोव्युष्टौ अवयक्ष्वनो वरुणग्ं
रराणो वीहि मृडीकग्ं सुहवोन ऐधि
स्स्वाहा अग्नीवरुणाभ्यांमिदं नमम

त्वमग्ने अयास्ययासन् मनसाहितः
अयासन् हव्यमूहिषे अयानोधेहि भेषजं
स्वाहा
अग्नये अयस इदं नमम

imam mē varuṇaśrudhīhava madhyācamṛḍaya tvāmavasyu rācakē svāhā varuṇāyēdam namama	O Varuna, listen to this invocation. Bring happiness to us now. I pray to you and seek your protection. This oblation therefore is Varuna's and not mine.
tatvāyāmi brahmaṇā vandamānastadāshāstē yajamānō havirbhi: ahēḍamānō varuṇēhabōdhyuruśagamsa māna āyu: pramōṣī svāhā varuṇāyēdam namama	Adored by many with Vedic mantras and homa samagris, O Varuna, increase our longevity. This oblation therefore is Varuna's and not mine.
tvamnō agnē varuṇasya vidvān dēvasya hēḍō avayāsisīṣhṭhā: yajiśṭhōvahnitamaśyōśucānō vishvādvēṣāgmsi pramumugdhyamat svāhā agnīvaruṇābhyāmidam namama	O Agni! You are the wisest and most splendid of all the gods to whom sacrificial offerings are made through you. Let Varuna be appeased and let all enmities cease. This oblation is Agni's and Varuna's, not mine.
satvannō agnē avamō bhavōtī nēdiṣṭhō asyā uṣasō vyuṣṭhau avayakṣvanō varuṇagm rarāṇō vīhi mṛḍīkagm suhavōna ēdhi ssvāhā agnīvaruṇābhyāmidam namama	O Agni you are the first among gods as described above. Be with us in the dawn and remain close to protect us from Varuna's ire. Help us obtain sacrificial foods to offer gods. This oblation is Varuna's and Agni's, not mine.
tvamagnē ayāsyayāsan manasāhita: ayāsan havyamūhiṣē ayānōdhēhi bhēṣajam svāhā agnayē ayasa idam namama	O Agni, please come close to your devotees and convey our oblations and bring us remedies. Thus this oblation is Agni's and not mine.

Mangal Phera/Laja Homa

This ritual following the primary homas has the bridegroom hold the right hand of the bride while together they walk around the agnikunda with garments knotted. We have interpreted the four rounds or circumambulations as dedication to the chaturvidha phala purushaartha (dharma, artha, kama and moksha.) As stated in the overview the first three rounds are dedicated to the first three aspects and the final round to moksha. The groom leads the bride and chants the mantras as the couple circumambulate the fire. When they return to the starting point they offer laja (puffed rice) to Agni. The fourth round, however, praying for moksha, is led by the bride. While a variety of havan samagris (materials for yajna) are offered in the primary fire ritual, during laaja homa only parched or puffed rice is offered. The bride's brother (or a friend) positions himself to one side at the head of the kunda with the bowl of puffed rice and fills the open palms of the bride with it at the end of each round. The groom adds a spoon of ghee to the handful of puffed rice in the bride's palms. As the mantras are chanted by the groom or the priest on his behalf, the bride offers the contents to the fire while the groom offers a spoon of ghee.

मंगळ फेरा/ लाज हॊम

तुभ्यमग्ने पर्यहवन् थ्सूर्यां वहतु नासः
पुनः पतिभ्यो जायादा अग्ने प्रजया सहः
पुनः पत्नी मग्निरदा दायुषा सह वर्चसा
दीर्घायु रस्यायः पतिस्स ऐतु शरदश्शतं *

इयं नार्युपब्रूते कुल्पान्याव पंतिका
दीर्घायुरस्तु मे पतिर्जीवातु शरदश्शतं स्वाहाः
अग्नये आर्यम्ण इदं नमम
वध्वै सूर्याय नमः

Repeat *

आर्यमणं नु देवं कन्या अग्निमयक्षत
स इमां देवो अध्वरः प्रेतो मुंजातिना
मुत स्सुबध्धा ममुतस्करथ्स्वाहाः
अग्नये आर्यम्ण इदं नमम

Repeat *

त्वमर्यमा भवसि यत्कनीनां नाम
स्वधावन् स्वर्यं भिभर्शि अंजंति वृक्षं सुधितं

नगोभिर्यद्दंपती समनसा कृणोषि स्वाहा
अग्नये आर्यम्ण इदं नमम

Repeat *

प्रजापतये स्वाहा
प्रजापतय इदं नमम

The mantra indicated by * is repeated before beginning each round.

Lājahōma	**Laja Homa**
*tubhyamagnē paryahavan thsūryām vahatu nāsa: puna: patibhyō jāyādā agnē prajayā saha: puna: patnī magniradā dāyuṣā saha varchasā dīrghāyu rasyāya: patissa ētu sharada śśatam [* Repeat]*	O Agni you received Sooryaa, the goddess and authority for wedding ceremonies in the form of bridal dower wealth. Now please bestow upon us that wealth and progeny through this bride. Agni has given this radiant husband with long life. May this bride's husband live for a hundred years.
iyam nāryupabrūtē kulpānyāva pantikā dīrghāyurastu mē patirjeevātu śaradaśśatam svāhā: agnayē āryamṇa idam namama vadhvai sūryāya nama:	This bride, while offering this oblation, prays for a life of a hundred years for her husband. This oblation is Sooryaa's in the form of this bride, not mine.
* *aaryamaṇam nu dēvam kanyā agnimayakṣata sa imām dēvō adhvara: prētō munjātinā muta ssubaddhā mamutaskarathsvāhā agnayē āryamṇa idam namama*	* Brides worshipped Aryama in the past and obtained husbands quickly. Let Aryama now effect her release from the family of her parents and help her enter her own family in a stable manner. This oblation therefore is Aryama's, not mine.
* *tvamaryamā bhavasi yatkanīnām naama svadhaavan svaryam bhibharśi anjanti vṛkṣam sudhitam nagōbhiryaddampatī samanasā kṛṇōṣi svāhā agnayē āryamṇa idam namama*	* Aryama! You are named Aryama since you have the power to unite partners in a firm bond. Bring the minds of this couple together with the strength of a well-fixed and firmly rooted tree. This oblation is for Aryama in Agni's form, not mine.
** *prajāpatayē svahā prajāpataya idam namama*	** Oblations to Prajaapati. This is Prajaapati's, not mine.

Saptapadi	**सप्तपदि**
Saptapadi, the ceremony of seven steps is the essential and pivotal element in a Vedic wedding. In law as well as generally held Hindu belief, the bride and the groom attain the status of husband and wife only after the seventh step is taken. Each step taken by the couple specifies that they be blessed with food, strength, ritual knowledge, love, welfare of cattle, prosperity, and sacred illumination. Either all the steps are taken at the northern side of the fire, sometimes by having the bride step into seven circles or mounds of rice, or the couple may complete the seven steps in a single circumambulation. The ritual begins with the couple standing with hands joined and with the agnikunda on their right. The groom leads the bride through each step forward, reciting the chant after the priest before each step. The paces are measured such that after the seventh step the couple is back at the front of the agnikunda facing the assembly. The groom chants or repeats after the priest:	सामामनुव्रता भव पुत्रान् विंदावहै बहूस्ते संतु जरदुश्टयः [*] ईष एक पदी भव –इति प्रथमं [*] ऊर्जे द्विपदी भव –इति द्वितीयं [*] व्रताय त्रिपदी भव –इति तृतीयं [*] मायो भवाय चतुश्पदी भव – इति चतुर्थं [*] पशुभ्या पंचपदी भव – इति पंचमं [*] रायस्पोषाय षट्पदी भव – इति षष्टं [*] होत्रेभ्यः सप्तपदी भव – इति सप्तमं

Saptapadi	Seven Steps
sāmāmanuvratā bhava putrān vindāvahai bahūstē santu jaradushṭhaya: [*]	Please follow me here. May we gain many sons and grandsons. And may they reach old age (live long). ***[This verse is repeated before each step is taken.]***
īṣa ēka padī bhava -iti prathamam	Take this first step for the sake of nourishment.
Repeat [*] ūrjē dvipadī bhava -iti dvitīyam	Take this second step for the sake of strength.
Repeat [*] vratāya tripadī bhava -iti tṛtīyam	Take this third step for the sake of ritual austerities.
Repeat [*] māyō bhavāya catuśpadī bhava iti caturtham	Take this fourth step for the sake of love.
Repeat [*] paśubhyā pancapadī bhava - iti pancamam	Take this fifth step for the sake of cattle.
Repeat [*] rāyaspōṣāya ṣatpadī bhava - iti ṣaṣṭam	Take this sixth step for the sake of prosperity.
Repeat [*] hōtrēbhya: saptapadī bhava - iti saptamam	Take this seventh step to be sacredly illumined.

Both the bride and groom chant or repeat after the priest the mantra *	* सखा सप्तपदी भव सख्यंते गमेयं सख्यंते मायोशः सख्यंते मायोश्टः
After the seventh step, the couple face the audience (bride on groom's left) and the priest requests that each repeat the following mantra:	पुरोहित
Then the priest puts a few grains of akshata on the bowed head of the bride and blesses her as shown:	साम्राज्नी श्वशुरो भव साम्राज्नी श्वश्रुशां भव ननंदारी साम्राज्नी भव साम्राज्नी अधिदेव्रषु
After this the agnikunda is removed.	
The priest instructs the couple to be ready to receive general blessings from the entire assembly. The priest instructs the audience to respond with "tathaastu" at the end of each of the seven phrases of blessing.	संप्रियौ रोचिष्णू सुमनस्यमानौ पश्येम शरदः शतं जीवेम शरदः शतं श्रुणुयाम शरदः शतं

sakhā saptapadī bhava
sakhyamtē gamēyam
sakhyamtē māyōśa:
sakhyamtē māyōśta:

purōhita

sāmrājnī śvaśurō bhava
sāmrājnī śvaśruśām bhava
nanandārī sāmrājnī bhava
sāmrājnī adhidēvrașu

sampriyau rōcișņū sumanasyamānau
paśyēma śarada: śatam
jīvēmā śarada: śatam
śruņuyāma śarada: śatam
[Vājasanēya Samhita]

With these seven steps may you become my friend.
May I deserve your friendship. May my friendship make me one with you. May your friendship make you one with me.

Priest

Be queenly with your father-in-law
Be queenly with your mother-in-law
Be queenly with his sisters
Be queenly with his brothers

Let us live as a loving, vigorous, happy couple enjoying each other's company, listening to each other for a hundred years.

आशीर्वादं

Ashirvadam/Blessings

This is the very final ritual step when the audience is requested to grant their approval to the blessings chanted by the priest by responding in unison with the word "tathastu" (it shall be so), as before, at the end of each phrase. These blessings combine melody and significance; they cover all aspects of the new life begun by the couple. The elders in both families as well as all friends assembled to witness the occasion have the opportunity to offer their final good wishes by uttering "tathastu." It is customary for everyone to offer (throw) akshata on to the heads of the couple but logistics and size of audience may prevent this practice. In that case the immediate families may do the honors as they say "tathāstu" while the rest of the audience may simply utter the word. Another option for the audience is to bless the couple with the akṣata as they walk down the aisle.

Final Blessings	आशीर्वादं
The priest instructs the couple to bend their heads down to receive the akshata. While the priest chants each phrase, the assembly responds with *"tathastu" 	स्वामिनः स्वस्ति मंत्रार्थास्सत्यास्सफला स्संत्विति भवन्तो महान्तो अनुगृह्णंतु अनयोर्दंपत्योः वेदोक्तं दीर्घमायुष्यं भूयादिति भवन्तो महान्तो अनुगृह्णंतु इमौ दंपती भास्करवदारोग्यवंतौ, मृकन्डवत् आयुश्मंतौ, कुबेर पुरंदरवदैश्वर्यवंतौ, सौभाग्यवंतौ, काश्यप सौभरी वत्संतानवन्तौ, भाग्याभिवृध्धि मुंतौच, भूयास्तामिति भवन्तो महान्तो अनुगृह्णंतु इमौ दंपती लोपामुद्रागस्त्यौ, अहल्या गौतमौ, अरुंधती वशिष्ठौ, शांता ऋष्यशृंगौ, अनसूयात्रि मुनिवराविव, सप्तपाकयज्न्य, सप्तहविर्यज्न, शतमख वरिष्ठानुष्ठानपरौ, चंद्रमती हरिश्चंद्रौ, दमयंती नळौ, सौभरितद्भार्याविव, तेजस्विनौ, वर्चस्विनौ, यशस्विनौ, भूयास्तामिति भवन्तो महान्तो अनुगृह्णंतु

Ashirvadam	Blessings
svāmina: svasti mantrārthāssatyā ssaphalā ssantviti bhavantō mahāntō anugr̥hṇantu *	O great assembled: May you grant that the good wishes bestowed on this couple be indeed true and effective!
anayōrdampatyō: vēdōktam dīrghamāyuṣyam bhūyāditi bhavantō mahāntō anugr̥hṇantu *	May you grant that this couple have a long life as enjoined in the Vedas.
imau dampatī bhāskaravadārōgyavantau, mr̥kandavat āyuśmantau, kubēra purandaravadaiśvaryavantau, saubhāgyavantau, kāśhyapa saubharī vatsantānavantau, bhāgyābhivr̥ddhi muntauca, bhūyāstāmiti bhavantō mahāntō anugr̥hṇantu *	May you grant that this couple enjoy as much health as the sun, as much longevity as Mrukanda, as much wealth and happiness as Kubera and Purandara, progeny as strong as those of Kashyapa and Saubhari, and increasing prosperity.
imau dampatī lōpāmudrāgastyau, ahalyā gautamau, arundhatī vaśiṣhṭhau, shāntā r̥syaśr̥ngau, anasūyā trimunivarāviva, saptapākayajna, saptahaviryajna, shatamakha variṣṭhānuśṭānaparau candramatī hariścandrau, damayantī naḷau, saubharitadbhāryāviva, tejasvinau, varcasvinau, yaśasvinau, bhūyāstāmiti bhavantō mahāntō anugr̥hṇantu *	May you grant that this couple carry out a hundred sacrifices including cooked sacrifices of seven forms with ghee as performed by the sage couples Agastya and Lopamudra, Gautama and Ahalya, Vasishta and Arundhati, Rishyashringa and Shanta, and Atri and Anasuya. May you grant that this couple be as illumined, as vigorous and successful as the couples Harishchandra and Chandramati, Nala and Damayanti, and Saubhari and his wives.

इमौ दंपती सुवाससौ, सुमनसौ, सुतापसौ,
सुवर्चसौ, निरंतर विधिहुत जातवेदसौ
निजतनु प्रभातिरस्कृत तमसौ,
अविरत नवनव दृश्यमान वयसौ,
हेलाविलसित वचसौ, मालालंकृत शिरसौ,
वेला विरहित यशसौ,
भूयास्तामिति भवन्तो महान्तो अनुगृह्णंतु

इमौ दंपती रोहिणी चंद्रमसौ,
रती कुसुमशरासौ लक्ष्मीपुरुषोत्तमौ, जानकी
रघुनायकाविव, परस्परानुरागयुक्तौ,
भूयास्तामिति भवन्तो महान्तो अनुगृह्णंतु

अनयोर्दंपत्योः अनवरत क्षेमस्थैर्य वीर्य
विजयायुरारोग्य सौभाग्यप्रदो भूयादिति भवंतो
महांतो अनुगृण्हंतु

इमौ दंपती श्रीवर्चमायुष्य मारोग्य
माविधाच्चोभमानं महीयते,
धान्यं, धनं, बहुपुत्रलाभं,
शतसंवत्सरं दीर्घमायुरिति भवन्तो महान्तो
अनुगृह्णंतु

imau dampatī suvāsasau, sumanasau, sutāpasau, suvarcasau, nirantara vidhihuta jātavēdasau nijatanu prabhaatiraskr̥ta tamasau, avirata navanava dr̥shyamāna vayasau, hēlāvilasita vacasau, mālālamkr̥ta śirasau, vēlā virahita yashasau, bhūyāstāmiti bhavantō mahāntō anugr̥hṇantu *	May you grant that this couple be always well clothed, of a similar mind, versed in practicing austerities, vigorous, always engaged in offering prescribed oblations to fire, radiant as light overcoming darkness, enjoying always new pleasures, eloquent in speech with ease, and successful without limit.
imau dampatee rōhiṇī candramasau, ratī kusumaśarāsau, lakṣmī puruṣōttamau, jānakī raghunāyakāviva, parasparānurāgayuktau, bhūyāstāmiti bhavantō mahāntō anugr̥hṇantu *	May you grant this couple to be mutually as passionate as Rohini and Chandra (Moon), Rati and Kama (whose arrows are flowers), Lakshmi and Vishnu, and Rama and Sita.
anayōrdampatyō: anavarata kṣēmasthairya vīrya vijayāyurārōgya saubhāgyapradō bhūyāditi bhavantō mahāntō anugr̥ṇhantu *	May you grant this couple everlasting wellbeing, courage, energy, success, health, longevity and prosperity.
imau dampatī śrīvarcamāyuṣya mārōgya māvidhācchōbhamānam mahīyatē, dhānyam, dhanam, bahuputralābham, śatasamvatsaram dīrghamāyuriti bhavantō mahāntō anugr̥hṇantu *	May you grant this couple abundance in luster, vigor, longevity and health and wealth of grains, money and progeny and a hundred-year life span.

Two more chants of blessing by the priest as follows conclude the ceremony, at the end of which the priest may announce the names of the couple as husband and wife. The couple may at that point prostrate in front of their parents and other elders in both families and the priest.

नवो नवो भवति जायमानोन्हान् केतुर् उषसां ऐत्यग्रम्
भागं देवेभ्यो वि दधात्य् आयन् प्र चंद्रमास्थिरति दीर्घमायुः

navō navō bhavati jāyamānōnhān kētur uṣasāmētyagram
bhāgam dēvēbhyō vi dadhāty āyan pra chandramāsthirati dīrghamāyu:

He, born afresh, is new and new for ever; ensign of days he goes before the Mornings Coming, he orders for the Gods their portion. The moon prolongs the days of our existence. (Griffith, *RV*)

This mantra is used very often in blessings. A liberal interpretation may convey blessing for an ever fresh, vigorous and long life. It is included here for its popularity among priests.

And finally another very popular blessing:

शतमानं भवतु शतायुः पुरुषः
शतेंद्रियः आयुष्येवेंद्रिये प्रतितिष्ठति

śatamānam bhavatu shatāyu: puruṣa:
śatēndriya: āyuṣyēvēndriyē pratitiṣṭhati

May you be (bestowed) with a life of a hundred years, with senses a hundredfold virile and may your longevity equal that of Indra (himself).

With this the entire wedding ceremonial/ritualistic parts are complete.

After this the couple may walk down the aisle to the previously designated location outside the wedding hall. The ushers may now point to the rows of audience for an orderly and safe exit.

APPENDICES

Appendix I: Materials

Appendix II: Rehearsal

Appendix III: Engagement Ceremony
Yagnopavitam
Kashiyatra
Grhapravesham

Appendix IV: Additional Wedding Customs and Rituals

Appendix V: Vedic Calendar

Appendix VI: Bridal Attire

Appendix VII: Ganesh Puja; Gauri Puja

Appendix I

FAMILY DATA FORM

Wedding Venue ....

Wedding Date.............. Time: .... # Guests.........Indoor/ Outdoor

Names:	**Bride**	**Groom**
Father		
Mother		
Paternal grandfather		
Paternal great-grandfather		
Gotras*		
Officiant(s)		
Phone/ email Mailing Address		
Dress**		
Transportation/Direction	Website/links	Address
Single Point of Contact	Phone	email
Rehearsal	Date/Time	Venue
Music/ DJ name	Live/CD/Other	DJ and/or Coordinator
Hotel name	Address	Phone/email
Ganapati /Gauri Puja Other Pujas	Date	Place

* Gotra defines one's rishi lineage. If a family does not know/remember their gotra, the priest may simply use the word "shubha" meaning auspicious.
** If there is a concern that akshata used during blessings may cause turmeric stains, alternatives such as using flower petals, plain rice or dry, lightly colored akshata need to be discussed.

Planning ahead:

Commonly in North America, couples locate and book a place of their choice for the wedding ceremony a year or so before the date. An early meeting between the priest/officiant together with the couple and their parents or stand-ins should also be arranged early. This meeting enables a systematic collection of the basic data as shown above, and is also the time to discuss family practices and develop a broad outline for the ceremony. It is best to agree that after a couple of iterations the program needs to be frozen and last minute changes avoided. For interfaith weddings, at least one meeting between the officiators is recommended in order to examine and agree to the logistics and sequence in order to make the process a seamless one.

Fire Ceremony Materials:

Havan or equivalent metal or metal-lined grille, about 18" x 18"
Small steady table, metal or tile-topped
Bricks or tiles, aluminum foil
Bunch of **dry sticks**; **paper**, 2 fire-starter cakes
Matchsticks, small candle, fire lighter

Havan samagri in a bowl
Puffed/parched rice in 4 small cups
Small jar ghee, with spoon
Sand in bucket.

Wedding Materials for Ritual Use:

Water in 1 pitcher or kalasha; extra bowl or smaller kalasha.
kumkum (red powder), 2 tablespoons.
haldi (turmeric), 4 tablespoons.
akshata (yellow turmeric-tinted raw rice), 1 lb.
coconut, one, decorated, to meet the groom or be broken by the groom;
coconut, second, lightly coated with turmeric for Kanyadanam.
fruits and flowers, 3 to 5 kinds; loose **petals**.
sweet or madhuparkam.
perfume sprinkler (optional).
Garlands (2), for bride and groom.
Also recommended: paper towels or napkins;
glass cover protection for deepas in outdoor ceremonies.

The above list covers the general minimum quantity of materials needed, most of them contained in the boxed list of items given below.

Preparing the akshata: stir a flat tablespoon of turmeric into a pound of raw white rice, with just enough water to coat the grains and to tint them yellow. The mixing should be done at least a day ahead to allow the akshata to dry.

Wedding Basic Materials List

#	ITEM	Function
4	Small tables	2 (approx. 26" x 24" diameter) to hold, store, & assemble materials during the ceremony; 1 (approx. 26" x 18" diameter); 1 (approx. 18" to 26" high) to support the havankunda, with fire proof or tiled top.
7	Plates (thalis)	2 plates of five fruits & flowers, 1 each for Groom's & Bride's side; 1 plate with garland for Bride's side to give to Groom who will later give it to the Bride; 1 plate with Bride's garland for the Groom; 1 arati plate (with kumkum, haldi, water, deepa, akshata, flower or spoon, madhuparkam or sweet); 1 plate of fruits & flowers to be taken with the Bride's entourage; 1 small plate with silk piece for the mangalasutra; (2-3 extra thalis should always be available. Fruits and flowers can be carried separately.)
2-3	Kalashas	1 decorated for procession to meet Groom; 1 or 2 for consecrating water for the ceremony.
2	Bowls	1 medium, to hold akshata; 1 large, to receive water at Kanyadanam.

#	ITEM	Function
9	Cups	1 ritual water cup with spoon (uddharana); 5 small, 4 with puffed or parched rice; 3 small, on arati plate, for haldi, kumkum, akshata; 1 small, for akshata.
6	Cloths	3 tablecloths; 1 large, for Antarpat ceremony; 1 small, silk, for mangalasutra
3+	Lamps (deepas), with wicks, oil	1 small, on arati plate; 1 or more for the Bride's entourage; (These may need glass mantle protection for outdoor ceremonies or use of battery-assisted substitutes)
2	Flower garlands	1 each for Bride and Groom (minimum; more may be needed for Swagatam or Milni)
2	Coconuts	1 decorated for Swagatam; 1 for Kanyadanam
1	Stone slab	For Ashmarohana

Sample Cover Page for the Program

ॐ

The Auspicious Vedic Wedding Ceremony

of

Chiranjeevi Saubhagyavati (Bride's name)....................................

Daughter of …………………………………….

and

Chiranjeevi (Groom's name)....................................

Son of ………………………………………………

Parthiva Shraavana Shukla Prathama
September…., 200X

Officiant: Dr. Amrutur V. Srinivasan

ऐकं सत् विप्राः बहुदा वदंति

ēkam sat vipra: bahudā vadanti
Truth is One, but the wise utter it many ways

Sample Program

Swagatam/Milni

While the guests are seated, the bride's family* greets the groom* and his family and friends, in a ceremony known formally as *Milni*. The priest blesses the groom, the bride's mother performs an *arati* (blessing), the bride's father garlands the groom, and the group returns to the mantap escorting the groom and his family.

Overview

The officiant* begins by giving an overview of Vedic wedding rituals. The assembly is reminded of its obligation/role as witness.

Veda Mantras

The ceremony begins with a recitation of Vedic chants. Purification mantras invoking the Sacred Rivers mark the mantap as a sacred space.

Vara Puja

The bride's father* declares his intention to welcome and honor the groom* and his family.

Jayamala

The bride* walks down the aisle with musical accompaniment. She indicates her choice by garlanding the groom. He garlands her to show his consent.

Pravara/Hasta Milap

The ancestral lineages of the two families are announced. The bride's father* unites the couple by joining their right hands.

Kanyadanam

The bride's mother* pours water over a coconut held by the bride, groom and bride's father which consecrates their union and symbolically passes their daughter to the love and care of her new family.

Mangalasutra

The groom* ties the auspicious necklace blessed by both families around the bride's neck, indicating his decision to marry her and her status of being married.

Exchange of Rings/Sindhoor

The couple exchange rings. The groom* applies sindhoor at the parting of the hair on the head of the bride.

Agni Homa

A sacred fire (*Agni*) is lit to receive offerings and to stand witness to the couple's vows.

Mangal Phera/Laaja Homa

The couple offer puffed rice to the fire as a symbol of the first hearth of their new home together. With garments knotted, the couple circle the fire four times, pledging to lead lives guided by *Dharma* (moral law), *Artha* (wealth), *Kama* (love) leading to *Moksha* (liberation).

Saptapadi

The bride and groom take seven steps around the fire, while they recite the customary vows.

Ashirvadam

Final blessings by the assembled conclude the ceremony. The couple seeks the blessings of all elders, family and friends as they embark on their new life together.

* May use actual names here.

The text of this Vedic wedding ceremony is arranged by
Dr. Amrutur V. Srinivasan of Glastonbury, Connecticut

APPENDIX II: Rehearsal

Rehearsal: Preparatory Steps

Stage Direction

At first glance one wonders about the need for stage direction in a religious ceremony. After all it is not drama. Upon some reflection, however, it should be clear that in a sense it IS drama, a real life one in fact, where the principals have specified roles that they need to "play" without missing a beat so that the series of steps do indeed blend together to reflect the meaning and symbolism of the culture and tradition of the families. Much time and money have been invested for many months by the couple and their families. Friends and relatives arrive at the ceremony with great expectation and excitement to watch the couple on their very special day. For these reasons it is important to designate one individual as the coordinator whose primary responsibility is to make sure that everything is in place as discussed during the weeks of planning and finalized at the rehearsal.

While the role of a wedding planner covers the preparations in terms of locating and booking the venue, photographer, videographer, selection of clothes, gifts, invitations, music and extraneous related activities up to and surrounding the ceremony itself, the role of the wedding coordinator covers the central event. The coordinator may be one of the principals: a parent, a friend or relative. He or she should be well acquainted with the entire ceremony. It is a given that the coordinator should attend the rehearsal and be familiar with the geographical setting of the wedding site in order to visualize positioning of all the steps both in space and time. The goal is a smooth flow of steps at the ceremony. This is possible with the aid of a knowledgeable or experienced coordinator.

The principals required at the rehearsal

- Overall coordinator, director
- Bride, groom, and their parents and/or stand-ins
- Bride's entourage (at least five young women from among the bride's family and friends)
- Bridegroom's best man and other groomsmen (at least five young men who will assist as discussed and identified during the rehearsal)
- Bride's brother(s)
- Five married ladies from the bride's family who will be in the processional to greet the bridegroom
- Fire managers (two selected from the groomsmen)
- Garland bearers (one from each side)
- A young boy or girl to collect water poured down during Kanyadanam
- Antarpat bearers (two selected from the groomsmen)
- Manager of mangalasutra blessing and akshata distribution (two selected from the five ladies above)
- Manager of sound/music/microphones
- Manager of pictures/videos
- Ushers (selected from the groomsmen and/or bride's family)
- Manager of the mantap: arrangements, arrivals/departures; clean up
- Hall manager

Rehearsal Plan

1. Set a time when all of the above can be present, preferably the evening before the wedding
2. Introductions of principals (the barat, bride's entourage, bridal family meeting the barat) by either the bride, the groom, a parent or coordinator
3. Determine locations and times (place where the bridegroom is to be met, place where the bride will start her processional, length of time needed to reach the mantap)
4. Set the time when the ceremony begins *
5. A description of what will take place step-by-step to be described by the officiant
6. Roles and responsibilities outlined
7. Meet at the site and walk through the main steps, discuss "difficult" steps, practice lighting fire
8. Assemble materials
9. Discuss role of Primary Coordinator (cues, communication, placement and movement of principals)
10. Understand when the ceremony begins and ends **

* The ceremony officially begins when the bride's party (priest, bride's parents, five ladies and any other group of elders and friends from the bride's side) assembles at and leaves the mantap and proceeds to receive the bridegroom and his party at the decorated gate or other designated location. This processional must arrive a few seconds earlier and wait for the arrival of the bridegroom's party.

** The ceremony ends when the officiator announces the couple as Mr. & Mrs......... and the couple descend from the mantap to seek the blessings of elders from both families, prior to walking down the aisle.

APPENDIX III

ENGAGEMENT CEREMONY

Introduction:

In the West, the time-honored practice is for the man, the groom-to-be, to ask his beloved, the bride-to-be, to marry him. This is often done in private, with or without the knowledge and approval of the families and is sealed with the gift of a ring to the lady. An engagement party may then follow. Such an engagement is considered a public announcement of the intention to marry.

The Hindu tradition also includes an engagement ceremony known as **Vāgdānam or Vākdāna** which means giving one's word (of honor). In fact it is an exchange of pledges by both families. The normal practice requires the families to assemble, approve and formalize the understanding between themselves or between the two young people. The words of honor or pledges are not exchanged between the principals but between the fathers. The bride-to-be and groom-to-be do indeed attend and participate, especially the prospective bride as she is welcomed and honored with gifts by the family of the groom-to-be. In this ceremony, in India, a ring may be presented to the groom-to-be by the family of the bride-to-be while the bride-to-be receives a set of jewelry and/or a saree and blouse.

Another version of the ceremony is common, especially in South India, and is known as **Nischitārtham**, the literal meaning being "firming up." The latter takes place usually the night before the wedding before an assembly of friends and relatives from both sides. The focus is very clear and the rituals become a part of the imminent wedding ceremony.

In any case, the magic of love or its prospect brings two young people together and that circle of magic expands, bringing together the immediate families and friends, in a joyous ceremonial event. The ceremony is based on

Vedic practices going back over 5,000 years. During the ceremony the basic "transaction" leading to the pledges is between the two fathers. This is done by proclaiming the lineages of the families and making a formal request for the alliance. Although there could be variations depending upon family traditions, one practice requires the father of the groom-to-be to make the first request. It is the affirmative response from the father of the bride-to-be that sets the stage for the remaining steps of the ceremony.

Materials needed:
Plates of fruits (five kinds), flowers, agarbatti, deepa with wick and oil, akshata, haldi, kumkum, engagement ring and/or saree and blouse piece, betel leaves, areca nuts, kalashas, raw rice, coconut, garlands, arati plate; paper towel roll, matches.

The Steps:
The following steps may be used with minor modifications depending on one's own family traditions.

1. A brief worship service to either Mahaganapati (Ganesha) or an ishtadevata (family's chosen godhead) performed by or in behalf of the GTB is followed by the father of the GTB greeting and honoring the family of the BTB. The GTB's father (or his representative) identifies the families to be united by reciting the lineage of both and expresses his keen interest in this alliance. The BTB's father responds affirmatively "after consulting his wife and elders in his family" ("*bhāryā jnātibandhvanumatim krutvā*" "भार्या ज्नातिबंध्वनुमतिं कृत्वा").

2. The GTB's family now greets and welcomes the BTB and offers a variety of fruits, flowers and garments (a new saree, and blouse). Additional gifts such as the engagement ring, bangles and necklaces may also be given to the BTB at this time. She may then be requested to go and change into the presented garments.

3. Upon her return, the BTB's father does a sankalpa and specifies this moment in space and time (see Appendix III) and declares his pledge and invites the GTB's father to sit or stand by the side of the BTB.

4. With the GTB's father standing or sitting by her side, the BTB's family honors the GTB's father while repeating the lineages and declaring that they give their word to this alliance in the presence of this "godhead, fire god and the families" (devāgni dvija sannidhau; देवाग्नि द्विज सन्निधौ). Note: Even though an actual agnikunda may not be present, the power of the mantras is considered adequate.

5. The groom's family accepts this word of honor and in a 21st century improvisation, shaking of hands and/or hugging by family members may seal the agreement.

6. Each father now expresses the wish that through this exchange of pledges each family will be happy.

7. The BTB and GTB are now each honored by members of the other family through an offer of garlands, and an arati is performed.

8. The ceremony concludes with blessings by the priest and the assembled.

The Ceremony:

The bride-to-be (BTB) is seated facing east; her father is to her left, her mother and other relatives to her right or behind her.

The officiant recites: अविघ्नमस्तु

avighnamastu

May there be no obstacles.

शुक्लांबरधरं विष्णुं शशिवर्णं चतुर्भुजं
प्रसन्न वदनं ध्यायेत् सर्व विघ्नोप शांतये

śuklāmbaradharam viṣṇum
śaśivarṇam caturbhujam

prasanna vadanam dhyāyēt
sarva vighnōpa śāntayē
I meditate on Vishnu, clothed in white,
the color of the moon, four-armed, of pleasant aspect,
so that all obstacles are lessened.

A prayer to Shiva whose very invocation is believed to clear out troublesome vibrations follows:

ओं नमः प्रणवार्थाय शुध्ध ज्नानैक मूर्तये
निर्मलाय प्रशांताय दक्षिणा मूर्तये नमः

ōm nama: praṇavārthaya śudhdha jnānaika mūrtayē
nirmalāya praśāntāya dakśiṇā mūrtayē namaha

I salute the Lord of the Southern direction who is the very embodiment
of the sacred symbol Om and of pure knowledge and eternal peace.

Invocation of Mahāganapati, family Godhead and Guru

With folded hands the officiant and the assembled chant the following:

करिश्यमाणस्य कर्मणः निर्विघ्नेन परिसमाप्त्यर्थम्
आदौ महागणपति स्मरणं करिश्ये

kariśyamāṇasya karmaṇa: nirvighnēna parisamāptyartham
ādau mahāgaṇapati smaraṇam kariśyē

So that the ceremonies we are about to undertake proceed
to completion without any obstacles we meditate on Mahaganapati.

गृहदेवतां ध्यायामि
ध्यानं समर्पयामि

gṛhadēvatām dhyāyāmi
dhyānam samarpayāmi

I respectfully contemplate our family Godhead.

गुरु ब्रह्मा गुरुर्विष्णु गुरुर्देवो महेश्वरः
गुरु साक्षात् परब्रह्म तस्मै श्री गुरुवे नमः

guru brahmā gururviṣu gururdēvō mahēśwara:
guru sākṣāt parabrahma tasmai śrī guruvē nama:

Salutations to the preceptor who is verily Brahma, Vishnu and Maheshwara and who personifies the Supreme Being.

Shuddhi (Cleansing)

The sacred rivers are then invoked to fill the metallic vessel. This water is used to cleanse and offer throughout the worship. Water is poured from one vessel into the smaller one while chanting:

गंगेच यमुनेचैव गोदावरि सरस्वति
नर्मदा सिंधु कावेरि जलेस्मिन् सन्निधिं कुरु

gangēca yamunēchaiva godāvari saraswati
narmadā sindhu kāvēri jalēsmin sannidhim kuru

O Ganga, Yamuna, Godavari, Saraswati, Narmada, Sindhu and Kaveri waters, please be present in this place

कोलंबिया कोलराडो चैव मिस्सौरि मिसिसिप्पी रियोग्रान्डे च हड्संच कनेटिकट्
नदीनां जलेः अस्मिन् सन्निधिं कुरु

kolambiyā kolarāḍō caiva missouri misisippī
riyōgrānḍē ca haḍsanca kaneṭikaṭ nadīnām
jalē: asmin sannidhim kuru

May the sacred waters of Columbia, Colorado, Missouri, Mississippi, Rio Grande, Hudson and Connecticut rivers manifest themselves here.

A spoonful (uddharane) of water is now poured into the hands of the principals who, while wiping their hands, chant:

अपवित्रः पवित्रोंवा सर्वावस्थाम् गतोंपिवा
यःस्मरेत् पुंडरीकाक्षं बाह्याभ्यंतरः शुचिः
apavitra: pavitrōvā sarvāvasthām gatōpivā
ya:smarēt puṇḍarīkākśam bāhyābhyamtara: śuci:
May anything unholy become holy, may all base tendencies depart,
cleansing both inside and out, as we recall the lotus-eyed Pundarikaksha.

GTB's father recites: ओं श्रीमन्महागणाधिपतये नमः
ओं श्री सत्यनारायण स्वामिने नमः
ओं श्री गृहदेवताभ्यो नमः
ōm śrīmanmahāgaṇdhipatayē nama:
ōm śrī satyanārāyaṇa swāminē nama:
ōm śrī gṛhadēvatābhyō nama:
Salutations to Mahaganapati.
Salutations to Satyanarayana.
Salutations to our family deity.

Pravara recital (reciting the lineage of both families):

प्रवर
त्रया ऋषयः प्रवरान्विताय .... गोत्रोत्पन्नयां ....प्रपौत्रायां, ...पौत्रायां,
श्रीमान् .... तथा श्रीमति सौभाग्यवति .... देवि पुत्रायां, चिरंजीवि .... नाम्ने वराय,

त्रया ऋषयः प्रवरोपेतां .... गोत्रोत्पन्नां ....प्रपौत्रीं, ...पौत्रीं,

श्रीमान् .... तथा श्रीमति सौभाग्यवति .... देवि पुत्रीं, चिरंजीवि सौभाग्यवति .... नाम्नी कन्यां,
भार्यात्वाय वृणीमहे

trayā ṛṣaya: pravarānvitāya .... gōtrōtpannayām ....prapautāryām, ...pautrāyām, śrīmān .... tathā śrīmati saubhāgyavati .... dēvi putrāyām, ciranjīvi .... nāmnē varāya,

trayā ṛśaya: pravarōpētām .... gotrōtpannām ....prapautrīm, ...pautrīm, śrīmān .... tathā śrīmati saubhāgyavati .... dēvi putrīm, ciranjīvi saubhāgyavati .... nāmnī kanyām, bhāryātvāya vṛṇīmahē

Descendent of three sages, born in the gotra …………, in behalf of the great grandson of ……………, grandson of …………………, son of ………………… and Saubhagyavati………………….., Chiranjivi………………………,

I ask for the hand in marriage of Chiranjivi Saubhagyavati ……………descendent of three sages, born in the …………….gotra, great granddaughter of …………………….. granddaughter of …………………..and daughter of ………………..and Saubhagyavati ……………

BTB's father:

वृणीध्वं, वृणीध्वं, वृणीध्वं

vṛṇīdhvam vṛṇīdhvam vṛṇīdhvam

It is my pleasure; It is my pleasure; It is my pleasure.

प्रदास्यामि, प्रदास्यामि, प्रदास्यामि

pradāsyāmi pradāsyāmi pradāsyāmi

I bestow her, I bestow her, I bestow her.

Vadhu Puja:

In this segment, the ladies of the GTB's family approach the BTB. Typically the GTB's mother picks up a plate of flowers, fruits, etc. and applies kumkum and haldi to the forehead of the BTB. This may be followed by a presentation of plates of gifts and garments. The BTB may be asked to change into the new clothing.

The families may now engage in additional pujas, chantings and songs until the BTB returns to the assembly.

Sankalpam/Declaration of Intention/Vaagdaana:

BTB's father sips water from the uddharana each time after chanting:

आचमनं
अच्युताय नमः
अनंताय नमः
गोविंदाय नमः
अच्युतानंतगोविंदेभ्यो नमोनमः
ācamanam
acyutāya nama:
anantāya nama:
gōvindāya nama:
acyutānantagōvindēbhyō namōnama:
Salutations to Achyuta
Salutations to Ananta
Salutations to Govinda
Salutations to Achyuta, Ananta and Govinda

शुभे शोभन मुहूर्ते, आद्य ब्रह्मणः, द्वितीय प्रहरार्धे, श्री श्वेत वराह कल्पे, वैवस्वत मन्वन्तरे, कलियुगे, प्रथम पादे, क्रौन्च द्वीपे, अमेरिका वर्षे, उत्तर अमेरिका खंडे, व्यवहारिके, चांद्रमानेनस्य षष्ठि संवत्सराणां मध्ये, ... नाम संवत्सरे, ...आयने, ...ऋतौ,............

मासे, ...पक्षे, ...तिथौ, ...वासर युक्तायाम्, ऐवं गुण विशेषण विशिष्ठायाम्
अस्याम् शुभ तिथौ, ...नामधेयह अहं मम धर्म पत्नि ....देवि सहित मम पुत्रि
चिरंजीवि सौभाग्यवति ....देवि नाम्नि करिष्यमाण शुभ विवाहान्गभूतं वाग्दानमहं करिष्ये.

śubhē śōbhana muhūrtē, adya brahmaṇa:, dvitīya parārdhē, śrī śvēta varāha kalpē, vaivasvata manvantarē, kaliyugē, prathama pādē, kraunca dvīpē, amerikā varṣē, uttara amerikā khanḍē, vyavahārikē, cāndramānēnasya ṣaṣṭhi samvatsarāṇām madhyē,.................. nāma samvatsarē, ………. āyane, ...ṛtau.................. māsē,.............. pakṣē, ...tithau,...........vāsara, yuktāyām, ēvam guṇa viśēṣaṇa viśiṣṭāyām asyām śubha tithau, ...nāmadhēya: aham mama dharmapatni .... dēvi sahita mama putri ciranjīvi saubhgyavati………… dēvi nāmni kariśyamāṇa śubha vivhāngabhūtam vāgdānamaham kariśye.

On this most auspicious time, in the earliest part of the second half of Brahma's term, of Vaivasvata manvantara, in the White Boar's millennium, in the first segment of Kaliyuga, in North America, in the general region of America, in the island of Krauncha (Heron), specifying, under normal practice, among the sixty Chaandramana years beginning with Prabhava …………………. year, ………………………. solstice, ……………season, …………………month, …………………….position of the moon, ………………the lunar day, ………………day, with such extraordinary time and day, I …………………………..along with ………………my wife in dharma, give this pledge as a part of the upcoming auspicious wedding rites.

Puja to the GTB's father: sitting/standing next to where the BTB's father is seated, the BTB's father offers him a plate of flowers and fruits.

BTB's father declares:

पूर्वोक्त ऐवं गुण विशेषण विशिष्ठायं अस्यां शुभ तिथौ मम पुत्री अस्य सौभाग्यवति .... नाम्नीं इमां कन्यां ज्योतिर्विदारिष्टे सुमुहूर्ते दास्ये इति वाचा संप्रददे

अव्यंगे अपतिते अक्लीबेदश दोष विवर्जिते इमां कन्यां प्रदास्यामि देवाग्नि द्विज सन्निधौ .... गोत्र ....नामधेयः वर विषये भवंतो निश्चिता भवंतु.

pūrvōkta ēvam guṇa viśēṣaṇa viśiṣṭāyām asyām śubha tithau mama putrī asya saubhāgyavati .... nāmnīm imām kanyām jyōtirvidāriṣṭē sumuhūrtē dāsyē iti vāchā sampradadē

avyangē apatitē aklībēdaśa dōṣa vivarjitē imām kanyām pradāsyāmi dēvāgni dvija sannidhau ....gōtra....................namadheya: vara viśayē niścitā bhavantu

As described previously, at this most auspicious time, I, in the presence of this godhead, the assembled elders and the fire altar, shall give this word of honor and bestow this young woman, my daughter Saubhagyavati ……………………, who is free of defects (perfect), single, healthy, free from any of the ten blemishes to proper alliance.

Acceptance by the father of GTB:

गोत्रोद्भवस्य ....नामधेयः वर विशये भवंतो निश्चिता भवंतु.

gōtrōdbhavasya ....nāmadhēya: vara viśayē bhavantō niścitā bhavantu.

In the matter pertaining to my son ……………………as the bridegroom born in the ………… gotra, it is now firm and settled.

Both fathers shake hands.

BTB’s father:

वाचादत्ता मया कन्या पुत्रार्थं स्वीकृता त्वया
कन्यावलोकन विधौ निश्चितस्त्वं सुखी भव

vācādattā mayā kanyā putrārtham svīkṛtā tvayā
kanyāvalōkana vidhau niścitastvam sukhī bhava

Having given the word of honor in regard to my daughter in this prescribed manner, please accept her for your son and be happy.

GTB's father: वाचादत्ता त्वया कन्या पुत्रार्थं स्वीकृता मया
कन्यावलोकन विधौ निश्चितस्त्वं सुखी भव

vācādattā tvayā kanyā putrārtham svīkṛtā mayā
kanyāvalōkana vidhau niścitastvam sukhī bhava

Having heard your word of honor in regard to your daughter, I shall accept in this prescribed manner and wish you to be happy.

Blessings

The bride-to-be is sprinkled with water and akshata by the priest and blessed with the following chants:

शिवा आपः संतु, सौमनस्यमस्तु अक्षतं चारिष्टं चास्तु दीर्घमायुः श्रेयः शांतिः
पुश्टिःस्तुश्टिः चास्तु ऐतद्वः सत्यमस्तु

ṣivā āpa: santu, saumanasyamastu akṣatam cāriṣṭam cāstu
dīrghamāyu: śrēya: śānti: puśṭi:stuśṭi: cāstu ētadva: satyamastu

May Parvati manifest here, may there be enjoyment, may she be secure, may she live long, prosper, be at peace, well nourished and content.

The bride-to-be may chant the following or repeat after the priest:

देवेंद्राणि नमस्तुभ्यं देवेंद्र प्रियभामिनि
विवाहं भाग्यमारोग्यं पुत्रलाभं च देहिमे

dēvēndrāṇi namastubhyam dēvēndra priyabhāmini
vivāham bhāgyamārōgyam putralābham ca dēhimē

O Indrani, dear wife of Indra, please grant me
a prosperous married life, and health, with progeny.

The ceremony is complete with the following blessings by the priest:

नवो नवो भवति जायमानोन्हान् केतुर् उषसां ऐत्युग्रं
भागं देवेभ्यो विदधात्य् आयन् पचंद्रमास् तिरते दीर्घं आयुः
navō navō bhavati jyamānōnhān kētur uṣasām ētyugram
bhāgam dēvēbhyō vi dadhyāty āyan pra candramāsthirati dīrghamāyu:
He, born afresh, is new and new for ever; ensign of days he goes before the Mornings
Coming, he orders for the Gods their portion. The moon prolongs the days of our existence.
(Griffith, *RV, ibid*)

शतमानं भवतु शतायुः पुरुषः
शतेंद्रियः आयुष्येवेंद्रिये प्रतितिष्ठति
śatamānam bhavatu śatāyu: puruṣa:
śatēndriya: āyuṣyēvēndriyē pratitiṣṭati
May you live a hundred years, with senses a hundredfold strong,
may your length of life equal that of Indra himself.

Yagnopavitam

Male children born and raised in traditional Hindu and orthodox families are initiated into the Vedantic fold through a ceremony known as Upanayanam. From a purely religious point of view this ceremony is a most significant step for a variety of reasons. First of all it ushers the boy out of childhood and in ancient times it meant that he was ready to begin the study of the Vedas under a guru in the latter's ashram abode. Secondly upon taking this step the young person becomes eligible to receive the most sacred and "secret" mantra of Gayatri as it is whispered into his right ear by his father in a climactic step. This eligibility is declared publicly when the boy is allowed to wear the yagnopavitam, the sacred thread made of cotton with a tight knot known as brahmamudi (knot of Brahma). This is deemed to be a life-changing event because the individual is initiated into a life of student celibacy with total focus on learning the wisdom of the Vedas. This lifestyle could continue through the rest of his life until and unless interrupted by consideration of the next stage of life defined as Grhastha (householder) as discussed in the section on Kashiyatra, a step preceding the wedding ceremony. The child initiate is termed a dwija (twice-born).

In the context of this book, if the groom has been thus initiated and if the family desires, then we need to consider the step in which he is required to wear the second set of the sacred thread that declares his new status in life, that of a householder. In this rite the initial three threads are increased to six. However if the groom has not already been through the first Upanayana ceremony and family tradition requires it, then that can be done the day before the wedding ceremony.

There remains the question of when to add the second thread ceremony. One possibility is to take this step almost after the Vara Puja. But a question may then arise about its rationality. The groom has not yet gone through the marriage ceremony after which the second yagnopavitam may be worn immediately. Immediately after what? Should it be after the tying of the mangalasutra or should it be when he has taken the seventh step of the Saptapadi which, according to Indian laws, confers married status. There lies a choice which the families involved may have to discuss and settle.

Investiture of the Yagnopavitam for the Householder

सन्कल्प

शुभे शोभन मुहूर्ते आद्य ब्रह्मणः द्वितीय परार्धे श्री श्वेत वराह कल्पे वैवस्वत मन्वन्तरे कलियुगे प्रथम पादे क्रौन्च द्वीपे अमेरिका वर्षे उत्तर अमेरिका खंडे व्यवहारिके चांद्रमानेनस्य षष्टि संवत्सराणां मध्ये ---------- संवत्सरे, ------------ आयने, -----------. ऋतौ, ------ मासे, ------ पक्षे, ------ तिथौ, ------ नक्षत्रे ----------वासर युक्तायाम्,

ऐवं गुण विशेषण विशिष्टायाम् अस्याम् शुभ तिथौ, ---------------

नामधेयह अहं मम गृहस्थाश्रम कर्मानुष्ठान योग्यता सिध्यर्थं श्वशुर दत्त

द्वितीय यज्नोपवीत धारणं करिष्ये. तदंग यज्नोपवीत परब्रह्म पूजां करिष्ये.

Sankalpam

śubhē śōbhana muhūrtē, ādya brahmaṇa:, dvitīya parārdhē, śrī śvēta varāha kalpē, vaivasvata manvantarē, kaliyugē, prathama pādē, kraunca dvīpē, amerikāvarṣē, uttara amerikā khanḍē, vyavahārikē, chāndramānēnasya ṣaṣṭii samvatsarāṇām madhyē, ---------- samvatsarē, ------------ āyanē, -----------. ṛtau, ------------ māsē, ------- pakṣē, ----------- tithau, -------------nakṣatrē, ---------------vāsara yuktāyām, ēvam guṇa viśēṣaṇa viśiṣṭāyām asyām śubha tithau, ----------------- nāmadhēya: aham gṛhasthāshrama karmānuṣṭhāna yōgyatā siddhyartham śvaśura datta dvitīya yajnopavīta dhāraṇam kariśye. tadanga yajnōpāvīta parabrahma pūjām kariśyē.

On this most auspicious time in the earliest part of the second half of Brahma's term of Vaivasvata in the White Boar's millennium, in the first segment of Kaliyuga, in North America, in the general region of America, in the island of Krauncha (Heron), specifying, under normal practice, among the sixty Chandramana years beginning with Prabhava ------------- year, -----------------solstice, ------------- season, --------------month, --------------- position of the moon, ------------------ the lunar day, -------------constellation, -----------------

day, on such superior time and particular day, I ----------------------, in order to attain the eligibility to perform duties relevant to the status of a householder, I shall wear the second sacred thread offered by my father-in-law. As a part of that I shall perform puja to the Supreme Being present in this sacred thread.

[Note: the specific sankalpam details for time and place given above are samples only.]

अस्मिन् सूत्रे यज्नोपवीत परब्रह्मणं आवाहयामि.
स्थापयामि पूजयामि. यज्नोपवीत परब्रह्मणे नम:
षोडशोपचार पुजां करिश्ये.

asmin sūtrē yajnōpavīta parabrahmaṇām āvāhayāmi. sthāpayāmi pūjayāmi. yajnōpavīta parabrahmaṇē nama:
ṣōḍashōpachāra pujām kariśyē.

I invoke the Supreme Being in the sacred thread. I install him and offer prayer.
I perform the *shodashopachaara* (sixteen part) prayer.

Here follow the same procedure as in the Ganapati puja replacing that prayer by yajnōpavīta parabrahmanē nama:

यज्नोपवीतं परमं पवित्रं
प्रजापतेर्यत्सहजं पुरस्तात्
आयुष्यमग्रियं प्रतिमुंच शुभ्रं
यज्नोपवीतं बलमस्तु तेज:

yajnōpavītam paramam pavitram
prajāpatēryatsahajam purastāt
āyuṣyamagriyam pratimunca śubhram
yajnōpavītam balamastu tēja:

This, the most sacred thread, is sanctioned by Prajapati Himself
and is considered sacrosanct.
This, the symbol of purity, shall enhance my longevity
and bring strength and vigor.

द्वितीय यज्ञोपवीत धारण मुहूर्त
स्सुमुहूर्तोस्त्वित्यनुगृण्हंतु
dvitīya yajnōpavīta dhāraṇa muhūrta
ssumuhūrtōstvityanugr̥ṇhaṇtu
May you please grant this moment when I wear my
second sacred thread to be auspicious.

The assembled respond with तथास्तु (*tathāstu;* It shall be so).

δδδδδδ

Kashiyatra/ Ritual Journey to Kashi

"This young man is well-versed in all the four Vedas and is now on his way to Kashi (Benares) for advanced studies in Brahmacharya" said the priest in the course of a wedding ceremony when the entourage led by the priest, the groom and his relatives were stopped by a group of people from the bride's side led by her father. The groom was clad in a dhoti which had been drenched in turmeric water and dried (sign of a holy person or mendicant) with a similar upper cloth worn on a bare back adorned with the sacred thread. A bundle, presumably packed with scriptures on the shoulder, a staff, sandals, an umbrella, a small water vessel added to convey the impression of a long journey.

It is a picturesque event and is indeed a part of most, if not all, Brahmin weddings to this day. A simple dialogue such as the one shown below accompanies this step in the wedding plans:

चरित ब्रह्मचर्योहं कृत व्रत चतुश्टयः
काशीयात्रां गमिश्यामि अनुज्नां देहिमे शुभां
carita brahmacaryōham kr̥ta vrata catuśṭaya:
kāśīyātrām gamiśyāmi anujnām dēhimē śubham

Please wish me well and permit me to proceed on my pilgrimage to Kashi
in order to undertake the four-fold penance of celibacy.

According to custom, this permission is sought from a stranger, here the bride's father, who interrupts the journey.

Then the bride's father steps forward to make his age-old appeal:

सालंकारां ममसुतां कन्यां दास्यामि ते द्विज
पाणिं गृहीत्वा साग्निस्त्वं गच्छस्वागच्छमद्गृहं
sālankārām mamasutām kanyām dāsyāmi tē dvija
pāṇim gṛhītvā sāgnistvam gacchasvāgacchamadgṛham

I offer you my daughter, fully adorned, in marriage. Please come to my home, hold her hand, partake in the fire rituals, and both of you may then proceed on your journey.

The sequence ends with an apparent acceptance of this offer as everyone turns around and proceeds towards the wedding hall.

δδδδδδ

GRHAPRAVESHAM
Ceremony at the New Home

Some families wish to conduct this step upon returning to their own home when the bridegroom's family formally receives the bride into their home or they may choose to complete the formality right after the wedding in a pre-designated section of the wedding hall.

Grhapravesham is performed when the new bride enters her new home for the first time. The format given below assures that she is now placed in charge of her own home or welcomed properly into her in-laws' home, where she ceremoniously makes her grand entrance blessed by the assembled.

The bride and groom along with her family (parents and other selected family members) approach the new home with Vedic chants and carrying plates of fruits, flowers, kalasha, uddharane, and deepa (lamp). The bridegroom's family stands ready to greet the bride and the groom into the new household.

The priest chants:

ओं नमस्सदसे, नमस्सदसस्पतये
नमस्सखीनां पुरोगाणां चक्शुषे
नमो दिवे नमः पृथिव्यै
सप्रथसभांमे गोपाय येचसभ्यास्सभासदः
तानि इंद्रियावतः कुरु सर्वमायुरुपां सतां
सर्वेभ्य श्री वैष्णवेभ्यो नमः

ōm namassadasē, namassadasaspatayē
namassakhīnām purōgāṇām cakśuṣē
namō divē nama: pṛthivyai
saprathasabhāmē gōpāya yēcasabhyāssabhāsada:
tāni indriyāvata: kuru sarvamāyurupām satām
sarvēbhya mahāntēbhyō nama:

Salutations to the assembly and its leader (presider), friends, family
and other notables present here. Salutations to heaven and earth.
May all the honorable and powerful belonging to the family, present or absent,
in this assembly be blessed with long life and be protected .

Just before entering, the bride and the groom should worship the threshold as follows by offering the upacharas, that is, by using akshata, water, incense, deepa, fruits, flowers. Begin with either or both mothers applying kumkum and haldi to the threshold as the groom begins to chant:

द्वारश्रियै नमः

dvāraśriyai nama:

Salutations to the goddess presiding over this entrance.

And continues with:

ओं इंद्राय नमः
ओं अग्नये नमः
ओं यमाय नमः
ओं नैरुतये नमः
ओं वरुणाय नमः
ओं वायुवे नमः
ओं कुबेराय नमः
ओं ईशानाय नमः

इति दिक्पालक पुजां समर्पयामि

ōm indrāya nama:
ōm agnayē nama:
ōm yamāya nama:
ōm nairutayē nama:
ōm varuṇāya nama:
ōm vāyuvē nama:
ōm kubērāya nama:
ōm īśānāya nama:

iti dikpālaka pujām samarpayāmi

Salutations to Indra, Agni, Yama, Nairuta, Varuna, Vayu,
Kubera and Ishana, the lords of the East, Southeast, South,
Southwest, West, Northwest, North and Northeast.
Thus I offer puja to the lords of these directions.

The groom may now do the sankalpam as follows:

पूर्वोक्त ऐवंगुण विशेषण विशिष्थायां अस्यां शुभ तिथौ
श्री भगवदाग्नया श्रीमन्नारायण प्रीत्यर्थं
नूतनागार प्रवेशं करिष्ये

pūrvōkta ēvamguṇa viśēṣaṇa viśiṣṭhāyām asyām śubha tiṭhau
śrī bhagavadāgnayā śrīmannārāyaṇa prītyartham
nūtanāgāra pravēsham kariṣyē

With the sacred features of the day as mentioned before, I shall now,
on this auspicious day, under the orders of the gods and to please the
supreme god Narayana, enter the new home.

The family group may now enter as music is rendered, with the bride leading, with her right foot inside first, followed by the groom and rest of the party.

The bridegroom recites the following Veda mantra (or repeats after the priest):

इह प्रियं प्रजयौ ते समृध्यतामस्मिन् गृहे गार्हपत्याय जागृहि
ऐनापत्या तन्वं सं स्पृशस्वाथ जिर्विर्विदथमा वदासि

iha priyam prajayau tē samṛdhyatāmasmin gṛhē gārhapatyāya jāgṛhi
ēnāpatyā tanvam sam spṛśasvātha jirvirvidathamā vadāsi

Version 1.

Happy be thou and prosper with thy children here: be vigilant to rule
thy household in this home. Closely unite thy body with this thy husband.
And may you both rule this house (give orders to your household).
(Griffith, Apte, RV. X. 85. 27)

Version 2.

Enter this your household to rule with vigilance. May you be happy
and prosper with offspring. Unite with your husband
and may you both be lords of this dwelling.

Previously sanctified water (See Sacred Rivers verse in previous Pujas, Appendix III) is sprinkled towards the four directions (east, south, west and north) and finally at the center with appropriate mantras shown below chanted by either the priest or the groom repeating after the priest.

ब्रह्मचतेक्षत्रंच पूर्वेस्थूणे अभिरक्षतु
यज्नश्च दक्शिणाश्च दक्षिणे
इषश्चोर्जश्पापरे मित्रश्चवरुणश्चोत्तरे
धर्मस्ते स्थूणाराज श्रीस्ते स्तूपः

brahmacatēkṣatranca pūrvēsthūṇē abhirakṣatu
yajnaśca dakśiṇāṣca dakṣiṇē
iṣaścōrjaśpāparē mitraścavaruṇaścōttarē
dharmastē sthūṇārāja śrīstē stūpa: (PP, 245)

Let this sprinkling [with sanctified water] be on Brahma
and his dominion on the eastern post,
this on the southern post south of the sacrificial fire,
this on the western post wishing wealth and vigor,
this on the northern post representing the Sun and Varuna,
and this at the center pillar representing the queenly dharma.

The ceremony may conclude with the following mantra chanted by the couple:

ओं सहना ववतु
सहनौ भुनक्तु
सहवीर्यं करवावहै
तेजस्विना वधीतमस्तु
मा विद्विशावहै
ओं शांतिः शांतिः शांतिः

ōm sahanā vavatu
sahanau bhunaktu
sahavīryam karavāvahai
tējaswinā vadhītamastu
mā vidviśāvahai
ōm śānti: śānti: śāntihi

May Brahman protect us both
May he bestow on us both the fruit of knowledge
May we both obtain the energy to acquire the knowledge
May what we both study reveal the truth!
May we cherish no ill feeling toward each other
Om Peace, Peace, Peace!

The bride is blessed finally by the priest with the following mantra

सम्राज्नी श्वशुरे भव
सम्राज्नी श्वश्रुवां भव
ननांदारी सम्राज्नी भव
सम्राज्नी अधिदेवृषु

samrājnī śvaśurō bhava
samrājnī śvaśruvām bhava
nanāndārī samrājnī bhava
sāmrājnī adhidēvr̥ṣu

Be queenly with your father-in-law
Be queenly with your mother-in-law
Be queenly with his sisters
Be queenly with his brothers

APPENDIX IV: Additional Wedding Customs and Rituals

Ankurarpanam
Anujna
Rakshabandhan/Visarjan
Sitting/Standing
Padaprakshalana/Ritual cleansing
Madhuparkam
Antarpat
Jeeriga/Bellam
Mangalashtak
Sitting on Father's Lap
Hasta Milap
Bride Moving From Right to Left
Tying the Knot
Ashmarohana
Vows
Talambralu
Ceremonial Presentation of Clothing
Dhruva/Arundhati Darshan
Sindhur Application
Drshti
Unjal
Games
Presentation of Gifts
Sashtanga/Blessings from Elders
Vidai

Ankurarpanam/Palikai

The day before a Vedic wedding ceremony, some families, especially Tamilians, observe a tradition in which a few sumangalis (married ladies) go through a ritual sowing of pre-soaked seeds in specially decorated small earthen pots containing fertile earth. It is common to use nine grains available in the region.

This ceremony is also called Palika Puja. The significance and interpretations vary. Some believe that eight of the grains are preferred grains of those gods that protect the eight directions of the future home of the couple. The ninth may represent the godhead that protects the center. Or the grains may represent the ones used in traditional Navagrahapuja. Another interpretation may be the expectation of potential new lives growing out of the union about to take place through the wedding ceremony. This is also an occasion in which, some believe, mother earth is worshipped. After the seeds sprout, the vessels are emptied into a body of water.

δδδδδδ

Anujna/ Role of the Assembly

At the commencement of an important ritual such as a wedding the officiator may seek permission of the assembled to proceed, in the appropriate Vedic verse. This requirement serves, not only as a mark of respect and acknowledgement of the authority of the assembled, but also implies their obligation to be witnesses to the wedding. Instead of down-playing this feature or taking it for granted, we have indeed integrated it into the ceremony and have benefited by using it at various times to keep the audience engaged. The audience is asked to grant permissions when sought by responding with a Sanskrit word "tathaastu" meaning "it shall be so." Thus religious mandates and rituals taking place at the sacred space are combined with the social approval of friends and family.

δδδδδδ

Rakshabandhan/Tying the Ritual Thread

In Vedic practice a turmeric–tinted yellow thread is tied on the wrists of the right hand of those who are performing a ritual. In that context the bride and the groom may wish to take this step at the time the pujas are performed the night before or on the morning of the wedding day. The thread is considered protective and stays on until completion of the entire ceremony.

Two versions are offered. The following mantras may be chanted by the bride and the groom.

Version 1:

गंगॆच यमुनॆच इत्यादि
अपवित्रः पवित्रॊवा इत्यादि

सुरक्षा दॆवताभ्यॊ नमः
ध्यायामि, आवाहयामि, आसनं समर्पयामि
कुंकुम, हरिद्रा चूर्ण, अक्षतां समर्पयामि,
नानाविध परिमळ पत्र पुष्पाणि समर्पयामि

रक्षा बंधन मुहूर्तस्सुमुहूर्तॊस्त्विति भवांतो
महांतॊ अनुगृण्हन्तु
ऒं त्रयंबकं यजामहॆ
सुगंधिं पुष्ठि वर्धनं
ऊर्वा रुकमिव बंधनात्
मृत्यॊर् मुक्षीय मामृतात्

gangēca yamunēcaiva ... ityādi
apavitra: pavitrōvā ... ityādi

surakṣā dēvatābhyō nama:
dhyāyāmi, āvāhayāmi, āsanam samarpayāmi
kumkuma, haridrā cūrṇa, akṣatām samarpayāmi,
nānāvidha parimaḷa patra puṣpāṇi samarpayāmi

rakṣā bandhana muhūrtassumuhūrtōstviti bhavānto
mahāntō anugr̥ṇhantu
ōm trayambakam yajāmahē
sugandhim puṣṭhi vardhanam
ūrvā rukamiva bandhanāt
mr̥tyōr mukṣīya māmr̥tāt

Tying the Raksha

Start with the invocation of the rivers and do the shuchi (cleansing) mantra as before:

Salutations to Ganga, Yamuna … etc.
May the impure be pure … etc.

Salutations to the godhead of protection
I meditate upon you, invoke you, offer you a seat here
I offer you kumkum, turmeric, akshata
And a variety of fragrances, leaves, flowers and fruits for your pleasure.

May the assembled grant this moment of tying of the protective thread
to be most auspicious.

Om. We worship the Three-Eyed Lord Shiva who is fragrant,
who enhances wellbeing. May he release us from death
as smoothly as severing a fruit from the vine.

Version 2:

अवयो: रक्षणार्थं रक्षाधारणं करिष्ये
नमो अस्तु सर्पेभ्योयेकेच पृथिवीमनु
ये अंतरिक्षेये दिवितेभ्य: सर्पेभ्यो नम:

अनयो: सूत्रयो: वासुकिं ध्यायामि
षोडशोपचार पुजा: समर्पयामि

avayō: rakṣaṇārtham rakṣādhāraṇam kariṣyē
namō astu sarpēbhyō yēkēca pṛthivīmanu
yē antarikṣēyē divitēbhya: sarpēbhyō nama:

anayō: sūtrayō: vāsukim dhyāyāmi
ṣōḍaśōpacāra pujā: samarpayāmi

We hereby wear the raksha thread to seek protection.
We salute all the reptiles residing on the earth, sky and the heavens.
We meditate on Vasuki, the serpent who can ward off all fears
and offer the traditional sixteen-step puja to him.

δδδδδδ

Raksha Visarjana/ Removing the Rakshsa

The practice is to undo the thread tied around the wrist of the right hand at the very end of the ceremonies. The following shloka may be recited while doing the visarjan.

सुरक्षा देवताभ्यो नमोनम:
कंकणमिदं विसृजामि विसृजामि विसृजामि

surakṣā dēvatābhyō namōnama:
kankaṇamidam visṛjāmi visṛjāmi visṛjāmi

Many salutations to the deity of protection
Let me the raksha thread undo, undo, undo.

δδδδδδ

The Question of Sitting or Standing

Should the ceremonies be performed with the principals sitting at the sacred space, as is the usual custom in India, or standing, which is the Western mode? Wedding rental companies generally supply throne-like chairs for the principals and other decorative seats for relatives and officiants along with the mantap.

The author's experience is that the structured ceremonies which he has conducted over the years are dynamic and that the movement of the principals and handling of ceremonial items during the ceremony are greatly facilitated by having everyone on their feet. Some steps such as the homas and Saptapadi require the couple to stand in any case. Furthermore the guests assembled have a better and clearer view of what happens on the raised platform or mantap. Due to their familiarity with wedding rites as conducted in other faiths, young people growing up outside India appear to prefer it. However, if traditon and nostalgia prevail, and the families prefer to sit down for most of the rituals, and stand where needed, that can be accommodated.

δδδδδδ

Pada Prakshalana /Washing of the Feet

Some families wish to observe this ritual in which a member of the bride's family (bride's father or brother) washes the feet of the groom upon his arrival at the entrance. Viewed in the context of the belief that the groom is the embodiment of Vishnu for the duration, one can justify the observance as a part of a Shodashopachara Puja (16-part offering) practiced when worshipping deities. If this is a final choice, then the groom can be asked to step into a brass or stainless steel plate large enough to accommodate the feet comfortably. Into this plate just enough water is poured to symbolize washing. If the family wishes to go through the actual motion of washing the feet, then the groom can step off onto a towel.

One variation is to simply dispense a few drops of water from the udhdharana towards the feet while chanting "padyam samarpayami" (I offer water for your feet).

With the shuddhi mantra (cleansing prayer) that will be chanted soon after the parties arrive at the mantap, there is enough justification to skip this step if desired as the spirit of cleanliness in every sense is met by the shuddhi mantra step.

δδδδδδ

Madhuparkam

Offering a sweet drink to the groom in a formal manner as he arrives at the bride's home appears to have been the practice in Vedic times. The particular drink referred to in the treatises on weddings is known as madhuparkam, basically a mixture of honey and yogurt.

Apart from the normal practice of offering a drink to a guest, any guest, the reason attributed to this particular concoction is its apparent nourishing quality expected to enhance one's strength and virility.

There is an elaborate ritualistic viewing of the elements (honey and yogurt) and chanting as they are stirred to mix. Dipping three fingers once into the vessel and using what adheres to sprinkle in the four principal directions and the center prior to drinking from the same appears to have been the practice. In some traditions it is the bride who offers the drink later, but here, as in most cases, it is her father.

In this day and age it is enough to symbolically offer any sweet or sweet drink as a gesture upon first meeting with the groom at the Milni. As there is usually a crowd accompanying the groom this appears to be an adequate gesture. It is best to include a plate of sweets in the paraphernalia carried by the bride's family welcoming the groom. This shows a clear intent. However, if one wishes, the groom may be offered madhuparkam itself.

δδδδδδ

Arrival of the Bride; The Antarpat; Garland Exchange

Some families practice a tradition in which the view of the arriving bride is shielded from the awaiting groom. Upon cue, two men (groomsmen) pick up a large piece of cloth (a saree for example), unfold it and hold it in front of the groom to obstruct the view of the bride from him. If this step is to be included, the chosen assistants are requested to hold up the cloth until the priest instructs them to remove it. With the previously selected music playing as the bride enters the hall, the bridal procession approaches the mantap where the bride is received by the priest and the entourage take places previously agreed to. The bride should stand facing the groom such that they are both visible to the assembly but not to each other.

The ceremony begins with the following mantra uttered by the groom and/or officiator:

आनः प्रजां जनयंतु प्रजापतिः
आजरसाय समनक्त्वर्यमा
अभ्रातृघ्नीं वरुणा
अपतिघ्नीं बृहस्पते
इन्द्रा पुत्रघ्नीं
लक्ष्म्यंतामस्यै सवितस्सुव

अघोर चक्षुर् अपतिघ्न्येधि
शिवा पतिभ्यस्सुमना स्सु वर्चाः
वीरसूर् देवकामा स्योना शंनो भव
द्विपदे शंचतुष्पदे

āna: prajām janayantu prajāpati: ājarasāya samanaktvaryamā
abhrātṛghnīm varuṇā apatighnīm bṛhaspatē
indrā putraghnīm lakṣmyatāmasyai savitassuva

aghōra cakṣur apatighnyēdhi
shivā patibhyassumanā ssu varcā:
vīrasūr dēvakāmā syōnā śamnō bhava
dvipadē śamcatuṣpadē

May Prajaapati bless her with children,
May Aaryama bless her jewelry,
May Varuna and Brhaspati protect her husband and his brothers,
May Indra protect her children,
May Savitar grant her wealth.

O Bride, may your peaceful demeanor and compassion provide peace in my family. May you bear brave children and bring happiness to both humans and animals. *(Griffith transl.)*

The priest concludes this step by chanting the qualities of the bride as follows:

संज्नानं विज्नानं जानदभि जानत्
संकल्पमानं प्रकल्पमानं उपकल्पमानं
उपक्लुप्तं क्लुप्तं
श्रेयोवसीय आयत्संभूतं भूतं
चित्रकेतुः प्रभानाथ्संभानां
ज्योतिष्मागं्स्तेजस्वानातपग्
स्तपन्नभितपन्
रोचनो रोचमान श्शोभन
श्शोभन कल्याणः

सुमंगलीरियं वधूरिमां समेत पश्यत

samjnānam vijnānam prajnānam jānadabhi jānat, sankalpamānam prakalpamānam upakalpamānam upakluptam kluptam śrēyōvasīya āyatsambhūtam bhūtam citrakētu: prabāhnāthsambhānām jyōtiṣmāgmstējasvānātapag stapannabhitapan rōchanō rōchamāna śśōbhana śśōbhana kalyāṇ:
sumangalīriyam vadhūrimam samēta paśyata

This bride possesses superior intelligence to bring harmony between the two families;
decisive, honorable, desirous of and ready to make a home. She arrives truly beautiful,
distinguished as a bright shining light, resplendent, charming, pleasing and lovely;
Hail this bride. Let all look at this bride who is auspicious.

Immediately after this chant the curtain is removed and the couple face each other.

A bridesmaid offers a garland to the bride while at the same time the best man assists the groom to take off the garland that is now on his neck. The bride is now instructed to offer the garland to the groom who in turn takes the garland in the hand of the best man and garlands the bride. With both garlanded now they face the audience with the bride standing to the right of the groom.

δδδδδδ

Jeelakarra-Bellum / Cumin-Brown Sugar

This is a tradition observed in some families and is considered a climactic event scheduled to take place at a time corresponding to the muhurtam (auspicious moment). Some families prefer this to be the first act upon arrival of the bride.

If the couple include this in the ceremonies, it is best to have them take this step when the antarpat is up. As the bride arrives and stands in front of the curtain, the priest instructs the couple to apply the paste of cumin seeds (jeera or jeelakarra) and brown sugar (bellam) to each other's heads reaching over the curtain or throw it over. This symbolizes that the couple will become inseparable much as the mixture of cumin and sugar, and also be ready to experience both the bitter and sweetness of life. The curtain is removed and they exchange garlands. The bride's parents now unite the couple by joining their hands.

δδδδδδ

Mangalashtak

Mangalshtak consists of songs in praise of the gods, praying for the well-being of the bride. They are traditionally sung upon arrival of the bride at the mantap. These eight verses vary from region to region in India.

The Bride Sitting on her Father's Lap

"Why did you not ask the bride to sit on her father's lap during the tying of the mangalasutra?" This question was posed a couple of decades ago by an elderly relative of the bride. This practice clearly originated during those periods when marriages took place between couples at a very young age and the step is still in vogue in some families. The practice is outdated these days when the principals are in their twenties and older. Furthermore, if the entire ceremony takes place with everyone standing, then this becomes even less relevant. Again, there is an element of nostalgia, of custom, and a father-child bond that may require the addition of what is now an option rather than a necessity.

δδδδδδ

Hasta Milap/ Joining Hands

Subsequent to Jai Mala or Jayamala (garlanding) and as the bride and groom turn to face the assembly, the bride's father steps up and places the right hand of his daughter in the right hand of the groom.

The groom is instructed to chant the following:

गृभ्णामि ते सौभगत्वाय हस्तंमया पत्या जरदष्टिर्यथाअसः
भगोअर्यमा सविता पुरंधिर्मह्यंत्वादुर्गार्हं पत्याय देवाः

gṛbhṇāmi tē saubhagatvāya hastammayā patyā jaradaṣṭiryathāasa:
bhagōaryamā savitā purandhirmahyam tvādurgārha patyāya dēvā:

(RV X.85.36)

O bride, I shall hold your hand in order to live long with you and our progeny through the grace of Aryama, Savitar and Indra who have granted us the status of householders.

(VP)

δδδδδδ

The Bride Moves from Right to Left

"I will come to your left if... "says the bride, extracting certain promises, during the wedding ceremony in some traditions. The basis for this procedure may be explained as follows: after the tying of the mangalasutra or a similar climactic step, it is the generally accepted practice for the priest to ask the bride, who up to this point stands or sits to the groom's right, to change sides. This possibly has its origin in the belief that Mahalakshmi, the consort of Mahavishnu resides in his vakshasthala, i.e. close to his heart, a stance which may be viewed in many pictorial and sculptural representations of Vishnu. In any case, this later step is also the basis for managing the early positioning of the groom and bride upon arrival at the mantap. It is best to guide the groom and his party to stand (or sit) on the left of the mantap facing the audience. When the bride and her party arrive, they are then stationed to the right of the groom's family. Thus when the indicated change does occur and she moves to his left, she has now moved from her family of birth to join her new family.

δδδδδδ

Gatha Bandhana/ Tying the Knot

It is common to tie the edge of the bride's saree or scarf or shawl to an upper garment of the groom to signify their bond before they circle the fire. It is best to have the couple repeat the following mantra during the tying.

बध्नामि सत्यग्रंथिना मनश्च हृदयं च ते
यदेतद् हृदयं तव तदस्तु हृदयं मम
यदेतद् हृदयम् मम तदस्तु हृदयं तव

badhnāmi satyagranthinā manaśca hṛdayam ca tē
yadētad hṛdayam tava tadastu hṛdayam mama
yadētad hṛudayam mama tadastu hṛdayam tava
(Sama Brahmana 1.3.89)

I shall tie this knot of truth to tie our minds and hearts together.
May your heart be mine and may my heart be yours.

δδδδδδ

Ashmarohana/ Stepping on Stone

Many families observe the tradition in which the bride is requested to touch a stone or step on to a stone slab with her right foot to emphasize the need for her to be a stable component of the new family. A small slab of stone may be placed for the bride to step on as she completes leading the groom on the last round of Laaja Homa. As this is a blessing the priest may chant the shloka as the bride touches the stone.

आरोहेममश्मानं
अश्मेव त्वं स्थिराभव
अभितिष्ठ पृतन्यतो
अवबाधस्व पृतनायत:

ārōhēmamaśmānam
aśmēva tvam sthirābhava
abhitiṣtha pr̥tanyantō
avabādhasva pr̥tanāyata:

Mount this rock here
Be as firm as this rock
In the midst of any conflict
Remain as stable as this rock

(ParasGS 1:7:1)

δδδδδδ

Vows

There are several Sanskrit mantras which can serve the couple as personal wedding vows and available moments to insert these into the program: directly following the Mangalyadharanam or ring exchange or before or after Saptapadi. The couple may exchange the vows directly or they may both repeat after the priest who can have them repeat the mantras in Sanskrit and/or the translations in English.

ऒं मम व्रतॆ हृदयं तॆ ददामि
मम चित्तमनुचित्तं तॆ अस्तु
मम वाचं ऎक मना जुषस्व
प्रजापति स्त्वानि युनक्तु मह्यं
पारस्कर गृह्यसूत्र

ōm mama vratē hṛdayam tē dadāmi
mama cittamanucittam tē astu
mama vācam ēka manā juṣasva
prajāpati stvāni yunaktu mahyam

(ParasGS 1.8.81)

Our hearts and minds, may they be one, may our words
delight each other. May divinity unite us both.

δδδδδδ

पश्यॆम शरद:शतं
जीवॆम शरदः शतं
शृणुयाम शरदः शतं

paśyēma śarada: śatam
jīvēma śarada: śatam
śṛṇuyāma śarada: śatam

(VS 36-24)

Let us live together in each other's sight,
In each other's company,
listening to each other,
for a hundred years.

अहमस्मि सहमानातो त्वमसि सासहिः
मामनुप्रते मनो पथा वारिव धावतु
सम्नौ भगासो अग्मत संचित्तानि समव्रता
यथा सम्मनसौ भूत्वा सखायाविव सचावहै

ahamasmi sahamānātō tvamasi sāsahi:
māmanupratē manō pathā vāriva dhāvatu
samnau bhagāsō agmata sancittāni samavratā
yathā sammanasau bhūtvā sakhāyāviva sacāvahai

May my mind move with your mind in love,
Let us move like flowing water on the path of life:
My life is linked to your life, my mind with your mind, my vows with your vows
Let us work together like two friends, like two seekers of the same goal.

(Lal, P., The Vedic Hindu Marriage Ceremony, 1996)

δδδδ

ओं क इदं कस्मा अदात्
कामः कामायादात्
कामो दाता कामःप्रतिगृहीता
कामः समुद्रमाविशात्
कामेन त्वा प्रतिगृह्णानि
कामेतत् ते
ओं स्वस्ति

(SSSRatnamala)

ōm ka idam kasmā adāt
kāma: kāmāyādāt

kāmō dātā kāma: pratigṛhītā
kāma: samudramāviśāt
kāmēna tvā pratigṛhṇāni
kāmētat te
om svasti

Om Who is giving to whom?
Love is giving to Love
Love is the giver and Love is the receiver
Love is the inexhaustible ocean
You come to me with love O Love, this is all your doing
Om All is holy

(Lal, ibid)

δδδδδδ

Talambraalu

This practice is common in Andhra weddings and appears to be related to the abundance of rice grown on the fertile fields of Andhra Pradesh, courtesy of the two great rivers Krishna and Godavari. In this ceremony raw rice is poured in large handfuls by the groom and the bride over each other's head in a joyful manner conveying prosperity and abundance now and for ever. It is best to play a musical selection which is joyous and vibrant while this takes place for about five minutes.

δδδδδδ

Ceremonial Presentation of Clothing to the Bride by the Bridegroom's Family

Some families have a tradition in which the bridegroom's mother presents clothing to the bride (a saree and blouse) after the Kanyadanam ceremony. The bride then retires for a few minutes to change into those clothes and return for the climactic step of Mangalyadharanam. Clearly this provides a break in the sequence and is an opportunity for a musical interlude or offering of song.

Dhruva Darshanam/ Sighting the Pole Star and Arundhati

Towards the end of the main ceremony, it is customary to include the step known as Dhruva Darshanam, the sighting by the bride of the pole star. Dhruva (Polaris) is seen near the constellation group known as the Saptarishi Mandala (Seven Sages; L. Ursa Major, the Great Bear) in Sanskrit. Because this star appears stationary at the same location irrespective of the earth's movement, Hindus have incorporated this feature into a ceremony where Dhruva is acknowledged with a prayer seeking such stability be granted to the bride in her new world.

The Sapta Rishis are the following: Kasyapa, Atri, Bharadwaja, Viswamitra, Gauthama, Jamadagni and Vasishta. This list may vary. The wives of these sages consider Vasishta's wife, Arundhati (also a star), to be a model of chastity, a pativrata. Therefore in addition to viewing the pole star, the bride is asked by the priest to imagine sighting yet another star in the sky, that is, Arundhati, and pray for a chaste life.

ध्रुवं ते राजा वरुणो
ध्रुवं देवो बृहस्पतिः
ध्रुवंत इंद्रश्चाग्निश्च
राष्ट्रं धारयतां ध्रुवं

dhruvan tē rājā varuṇō
dhruvam dēvō bṛhaspati:
dhruvanta indraṣāgniṣca
rāṣtram dhārayatām dhruvam
(RV X. 173. 5)

Steadfast, may Varuna the king,
Steadfast, the god Brhaspati,
Steadfast, may Indra, steadfast too,
May Agni keep thy reign steadfast.
(tr. Griffith, 1896)

Bride's prayer addressing Dhruva:

ध्रुवमसि ध्रुवाहं पतिकुले भूयासं
dhruvamasi dhruvāham patikulē bhūyāsam
You are forever stable. May I be as stable in my husband's home.

δδδδδδ

Sindhura Danam/ Sindhur Application

A practice prevalent in many North Indian families is the application of sindhur (vermillion powder similar to kumkum) by the groom to the hair parting on the bride's head. Some use a coin, slightly wetted, so that the powder adheres to its rim which is drawn over the parting for easy transfer. This is done close to the end of the ceremony. An appropriate mantra is the following:

सुमंगलीरियं वधूरिमां
समेत पश्यत
सौभाग्यमस्यै दत्वायाथास्तं विपरेतन
sumangalīriyam vadhūrimām
samēta paśyata
saubhāgyamasyai datvāyāthāstām viparētana

May good fortune attend this bride. Gather here one and all
and bless her before you depart.

δδδδδδ

Drshti/Warding off the Evil Eye

Those who grew up in villages in India will undoubtedly recall the fear of some mothers that children might be subjected to the peril known as the "evil eye" and consequently suffer illnesses, injuries or even death. This is an inherited belief and weakness prevalent in many ancient cultures and in India was given prompt attention after a young person returned from outside the home.

One of the several methods practiced in South India was to take a handful of red chilies held tightly in the right hand and move the hand in front of the "victim" three times in a large circle clockwise as if performing an arati. After the last round the entire contents in the hand are thrown on to the fire in the kitchen on which some cooking might be in progress. Lo and behold, the individual was now freed from any possible harm! The procedure was declared to be especially successful if the resulting smoke, which under ordinary circumstances would result in fumes and coughs, produced no such effects on the onlookers. Everyone was satisfied and life returned to normal.

Another example is to use a coconut, instead of red chilis, shattering the same after the third round. This is commonly practiced when a deity is taken out in procession around the village or when a groom/bride/couple return from a similar procession. The offering and shattering of watermelons in front of new cars or farm vehicles (during the Dasara festival) is part of this custom. Similarly one sees very often, especially in villages, a small black dot on the cheek of a child dressed up for the day. The theory is that bad disturbances are distracted by the sight of this "blemish" and minimized.

These ideas have naturally crept into wedding ceremonies although the practice is gradually disappearing. Because the bride and the groom are always especially attractive in their wedding attire (as is evident from the appended photographs!), it is not uncommon to see a variety of practices even now. Sometimes, a group of ladies will approach the couple near the end of the ceremony with a vessel containing colorful rice balls and go through the same motion described above. The rice balls are supposed to draw in the evil designs and are later discarded. If the families wish this step to be included in the ceremonies, it is best to allow them the practice before the final blessings. It is recommended that some music be chosen to play while this goes on for a few minutes at the mantap.

δδδδδδ

Unjal/ Oonjal

Unjal is a ceremony popular among South Indians and sometimes discussed in the course of planning a wedding. This is a practice in which women take a special interest and sing a variety of songs appropriate to the occasion while the couple swing gently back and forth, seated on a swing. Flower petals may be sprinkled on the couple while they swing. It is not uncommon for relatives and friends to persuade other young couples to take turns on the swing in a joyous celebration by the whole group of families. This practice may have its origin in certain sevas (service) offered to deities at major temples. Special halls are built outside for this very purpose where a divine couple, Rama and Sita, Krishna and Rukmini, Srinivasa and Padmavati, for example, are taken in procession, seated on a swing, and swung gently to music rendered by the devotees and/or the nadaswaram ensemble at the temple.

δδδδδδ

Games

In arranged marriages, not so long ago, when the young people to be wedded were virtual strangers to each other and when wedding ceremonies and entertainment were conducted over a week, it was customary to include certain games. These games might include throwing flower balls at or to each other. They involved mock fights or tests over snatching a ring out of a tray/vessel filled with water or rice or milk. They could include mutual feeding of sweets or pouring rice over each other. Pouring bowls of rice on each other's heads is discussed in Talambralu. Relatives of the bride may "steal" the groom's shoes and demand a "ransom" for returning the same! Understanding that there may be a nostalgic need to see the couple play these games, we recommend that they take place before or after the formal ceremony. There is often ample opportunity for more fun, music and dance in the days and hours leading up to the wedding.

δδδδδδ

Presentation of Gifts

Some families have the custom of presenting gifts to the couple at the mantap as a part of the ceremony. It is recommended that this practice be restricted to immediate family members. Some relevant songs or performances could be added concurrently here.

Sashtanga / Blessings from Elders

Sashtanga or prostration before the elders in the family and the priest seeking their blessings is a traditional Hindu way of receiving merit after any major ritual. If the couple chooses to observe this, then right after the announcement of their names as husband and wife, they may be directed to prostrate before the priest and previously designated elders from both families, beginning with the eldest. The elders in turn may throw a few grains of akshata on the heads of both, and touch the couple's heads with both hands.

δδδδδδ

Vidai/ Farewell to the Bride

A practice commonly observed in Gujarati weddings is bidding goodbye to the bride at the end of the ceremony. Even though she may not actually be leaving for her new home at that moment, her departure is observed symbolically. Members of the bride's family conduct her to the entrance door of the wedding hall and perform the send-off formalities (hugs and kisses, etc.) and let her leave with a plate of flowers, fruits and sweets in the company of the groom. Normally the couple enter a decorated car and go around the building and return to the same entrance which now serves as the entrance to her new home. The priest may then have them do the puja to the threshold and follow the procedures outlined in the Grhapravesham ceremony described in Appendix III.

Appendix V: Vedic Calendar

Hindu Concept of Time

Hindu belief in regard to time is that it has no beginning and it has no end. It is an infinitely long continuous flow cycle that is periodic with creation, movement, rest, end of epoch, dissolution, rest and then a re-creation with a continuous repetition of the whole cycle. In human terms it can be compared to the soul leaving a body upon death of the physical being and entering a new body after a period of rest to begin a new earthly existence, living an active life and then ending it to continue the cycle. We do not include here those perfected souls who attain moksha (salvation) and simply pass beyond the end of the cycle as they merge with the supreme Soul.

Reverence for nature has always been reflected in Hindu ritual. Invocation of sacred rivers and fire, references to the year, month, day, season, position and phase of the moon are all integrated into the specification of time and space necessary for a religious ceremony. The reckoning of time was based on the movements of the principal planets that could be observed. Further, ancient Hindus believed that the life of human beings is, to some extent, influenced by the position and movement of planets.

Sankalpa/Specification of Time for a Rite

At the beginning of a sacred ceremony, the officiant/priest and/or the person sometimes addressed as yajamaana (leader) who is conducting or sponsoring the rite must declare its position in time and space in order for the invoked godhead or deities to appear and be present in the objects of veneration (puja), and/or to sanctify the rite and to grant the blessings sought. A sacred space is delineated. In the case of a wedding, this space is the mantap. The declaration is called the sankalpa.

In a wedding ceremony, this important step known as sankalpa (declaration of intention), the location in time and space is to be specified by the giver of the bride. The basis of this specification is the Hindu reckoning of time and is referenced to the creator Brahma's day as will be defined below. The parameters used to precisely state the time are kalpa, manvantara, yuga, pada, samvatsara, aayana, rutu, maasa, paksha, tithi and vaasara.

While the ideal life span for humans is generally desired to be a hundred years, the time span for the creation cycle is on a different and vast scale. For example, Hindus reckon that a 100,000 years is a mere second in Brahma's time frame. With this scale in mind, we may define the length of time for the terms used in identification of time and space in the sankalpa specification as follows:

Brahma's day and life span:

1 daytime of Brahma = 14 Manus = 1,000 chatur yugas = 4,320,000,000 solar years.
1 night time of Brahma = 4,320,000,000 solar years, during which Brahma rests.
1 year of Brahma = 365 days x 8,640,000,000 solar years.
1 life span of Brahma = 100 x 365 days x 8,640,000,000 solar years.

When Brahma rests at night, during each kalpa, the three worlds (Bhuloka, Bhuvarloka & Suvarloka) are dissolved in a deluge (pralaya); when his life span ends, all seven worlds will perish. When a life span of Brahma ends, the cosmos ends but Brahman remains; another Brahma will begin the task of creation and the cycles will repeat.

Para = half of Brahma's term

Kalpa = day of Brahma = 4,320,000,000 years (four billion and three hundred twenty million years). We are now in what is known as Shweta Varaaha Kalpa, an epoch which belongs in the second half of the life of Brahma. According to the purana after which the kalpa is named, Lord Varaha (an incarnation of Vishnu) is said to have emerged from Brahma that day in the form of a white boar in order to rescue Bhu Devi (Mother Earth) from the deluge of that age and kalpa.

Manvantara = the period in the active daytime of Brahma ruled by a Manu. The current manvantara is ruled by a Manu known as Vaivasvata. The fourteen Manus who follow each other during a daytime of Brahma are: Swayambhuva, Sawosisha, Audhama, Thamasa, Raivatha, Sakshusha, Vaivasvata, Savarni, Daksha Savarni, Brahma Savarni, Dharma Savarni, Rudra Savarni, Rouchya and Bowdhya. The present Kali Yuga is said to be the 28th in the present seventh, Vaivasvata Manvantara.

Yuga = one of four ages, often referred to in the epics and puranas or story cycles of the gods. Kali Yuga, a span of 432,000 years, is the current yuga.

One day in the life-span of the divine creator Brahma is considered to be equivalent to 1,000 cycles of the four yugas or chaturyugas. The yugas consist of Krta or Satya Yuga, lasting 1,728,000 solar years, Treta Yuga, a duration of 1,296,000 years, Dwapara Yuga 834,000 years, and Kali, the present yuga, of 432,000 human years. One cycle of the above four yugas is one mahayuga or divya yuga of 4.32 million solar years. Hindu astronomy identifies the current Kali Yuga (Iron Age) as beginning at midnight between February 17 & 18, 3102 B.C.

Pada = part of Brahma's day. Prathama pada is the first division of Dvitiya Parardha (second half) of the life of Brahma.

Aayana = the time period dominated by the direction of the sun. Uttarayana begins when the sun changes direction and begins his "journey" northwards on Makara Sankranti day. When the direction of the sun's travel appears to be southern, away from the northern hemisphere, it is Dakshinaayana.

Paksha = fortnightly phase of moon. Upon passing the new moon day, the paksha becomes Shukla (bright) as the moon waxes, and upon passing the full moon day, the paksha becomes Krishna (dark), as the moon wanes .

Ritu (Rutu) = season (the 6 seasons of the 12 months in the lunar year as shown in the list below):

Shishira (Late winter: January and February), *Vasanta* (Spring: March and April)
Greeshma (Summer: May and June), *Varsha* (Rainy: July and August)
Sharad (Fall: September and October), *Hemanta* (Early winter: November and December)

Samvatsara = year. The Hindu years or samvatsaras repeat in a cycle of 60 as shown in the table below:

Prabhava	1987--1988	*Hevilambi*	2017--2018
Vibhava	1988--1989	*Vilambi*	2018--2019
Shukla	1989--1990	*Vikari*	2019--2020
Pramoduta	1990--1991	*Sharvari*	2020--2021
Prajotpatti	1991--1992	*Plava*	2021--2022
Angirasa	1992--1993	*Shubakritu*	2022--2023
Srimukha	1993--1994	*Shobakritu*	2023--2024
Bhava	1994--1995	*Krodhi*	2024--2025
Yuva	1995--1996	*Vishvavasu*	2025--2026
Dhatu	1996--1997	*Parabhava*	2026--2027
Isvara	1997--1998	*Plavanga*	2027--2028
Bahudhanya	1998--1999	*Kilaka*	2028--2029
Pramathi	1999--2000	*Saumya*	2029--2030
Vikrama	2000--2001	*Sadharana*	2030--2031
Vishu	2001--2002	*Virodhikritu*	2031--2032
Chitrabanu	2002--2003	*Paridhavi*	2032--2033
Svabhanu	2003--2004	*Pramadhicha*	2033--2034
Tarana	2004--2005	*Ananda*	2034--2035
Parthiva	2005--2006	*Rakshasa*	2035--2036
Vyaya	2006--2007	*Nala*	2036--2037
Sarvajit	2007--2008	*Pingala*	2037--2038
Sarvadhari	2008--2009	*Kalayukti*	2038--2039
Virodhi	2009--2010	*Siddharthi*	2039--2040
Vikruti	2010--2011	*Raudri*	2040--2041
Khara	2011--2012	*Durmati*	2041--2042
Nandana	2012--2013	*Dundubhi*	2042--2043
Vijaya	2013--2014	*Rudhirodgari*	2043--2044
Jaya	2014--2015	*Raktakshi*	2044--2045
Manmatha	2015--2016	*Krodhana*	2045--2046
Durnmukhi	2016--2017	*Akshaya*	2046--2047

Maasa = Month.

There are 12 maasas in a year, lunar or solar. Since the lunar year is shorter than the solar year by about 11 days, once every 3 lunar years, an additional lunar month is added to realign with the solar year. It is called 'Adhika Maasa'. In other words, one of the lunar months will repeat.

Tithi = lunar day; this is the time it takes for the longitudinal angle between the moon and the sun to increase by 12 degrees. When the Sun and Moon are at the same longitude, it is Amavasya or new moon and when they are 180 degrees apart it is Poornima or full moon. In each paksha there are 15 tithis for a total of 30 tithis in a lunar month. The 15th thithi of Shukla Paksha is Poornima and the 15th of Krishna Paksha is Amavasya. Apart from the new moon and full moon, the other 14 tithis in each Paksha have the same names, which are literally numbers expressed in Sanskrit, from one through fourteen, i.e. Prathama, Dwiteeya, (First, Second, etc.), Triteeya, Chaturthi, Panchami, Shashti, Saptami, Ashtami, Navami, Dashami, Ekaadashi, Dwaadashi, Trayodashi, and Chaturdashi.

Vaasara = the day of the week; the names are adopted after the pattern of Western time-keeping:

Rahukalam

An added feature in the selection of time of the ceremony is to avoid what is known as the time of Rahu which varies from day to day. While this particular time is readily available in Hindu almanacs, a general appreciation of how it is calculated is stated briefly here. The daily difference between the sunrise and sunset hours is determined for the region. This is divided into 8 segments and the first segment is discarded. The second interval is the Rahukaalam for Monday (generally around 7:30 a.m. to 9:00 a.m.), the third and successive segments are assigned to Saturday (9 a.m. to 10:30 a.m.), Friday (10:30 a.m. to 12 noon), Wednesday (12 noon to 1:30 p.m.), Thursday (1:30 p.m. to 3:00 p.m.), Tuesday (3:00 p.m. to 4:30 p.m.) and Sunday (4:30 p.m. to 6:00 p.m.).

Sample Sankalpam

On this most auspicious time in the earliest part of the second half of Brahma's term of Vaivasvata in the White Boar's millennium, in the first segment of Kaliyuga, in North

America, in the general region of America, in the island of Krauncha (Heron), specifying, under normal practice, among the sixty Chaandramana years beginning with Prabhava, ... year, ...course of the sun, ... season, ... month, ... position of the moon, ... lunar day, ... constellation, ... day, with such extraordinary time and day, I, ..., along with .... my wife in dharma, declare my intention to welcome this bridegroom, ..., born in ....gotra and his family in order to offer Vara Puja in connection with the auspicious wedding of my daughter, Chiranjeevi Saubhaagyavati .... Devi.

Additional Sankalpam: When families request the traditional approach in which the sankalpa is done before Vara Puja and later repeated at the time of Kanyadaanam, only the wording pertaining to the specific step needs to be changed or included.

Sankalpam/Specification of Place for a Rite

Generally only the greater region is specified as, for example, "bharata varshe bharata khande" in India. In North America similar reference is made by specifying "amerika varshe uttara amerika khande." If one wishes to include the local region (state/province, city etc.) that is acceptable. Krauncha is one of the seven island-continents or dvipas that constitute the land-mass of the earth in Hindu mythology. It is situated west of Mount Meru. Meru, or Sumeru, the pivotal mountain at the center of the earth is located north of India (Bharatavarsha), possibly at the north pole. Because the sun was said to circle this mountain every day it has also been claimed by Hindu and Buddhist legend to be the center of the universe. Traditionally is is the home of the gods, Brahma in particular. The western location of Krauncha in respect to this mountain has made it a popular reference for sankalpams declared in North America.

Horoscopes

While it is true that ancient Hindus focused inwards while trying to unravel the mysteries of the self in their quest of the greater Self, they also turned their attention to the study of the outer universe. Thus the interest in constellations and the heavens, their relationships, and their influence on individual lives. Such influence was calculated on the basis of the position of planets at the precise time of birth of individuals. In a sense, one could look upon a life as being launched into a dynamic system, and the subsequent "movement" of that living system depended upon the initial conditions of the total system. This is what led to the writing of horoscopes, which sought to establish the general characteristics of the individual's life. It was an ingenious method of acknowledging our connection and linking our fate and fortune with the larger universe.

The positions of Surya (Sun), Chandra (Moon), Angaraka (Mars), Budha (Mercury), Guru (Jupiter), Shukra (Venus), Shani (Saturn) along with those of the "sub-planets" or malign influences, Rahu and Ketu, at the time of birth of an individual define the horoscope. Millions of Hindu families still consult a priest to have the horoscopes of the bride and groom studied in order to determine the probable influence of one course of life on another as predicted by the planetary positions and thus to project the compatibility of the union. It is part of the screening process in an arranged marriage, but is generally ignored in the case of marriages made by choice or interfaith marriages.

Appendix VI: Indian Bridal Attire

1. Indian Bridal Jewelry

As befits a civilization that traded textiles, gold and gemstones to the Roman Empire, India still places an emphasis on these accessories to a wedding. Bridal attire is resplendent with color, richness of fabric, and adornments in jewels from head to toe.

The ancient tradition of *Sola shringaar* or the sixteen traditional adornments for all parts of the body may still be a step in in the preparations for a Rajasthani wedding, but it can be expected to make an appearance at any wedding:

"I offer you my daughter, standing by my side, foremost among young women, covered in jewels,…" says the would-be father-in-law in that well known line from the wedding ceremony.

This jewelry was, historically, a large part of the Indian bride's dower, her "stridhan," and on her wedding day she might wear essentially all of it. In fact the variety of bangles, earrings, necklaces, armlets, nose-pins, rings (for fingers and toes) in sets and unique pieces is so vast and generally available that only jewelry that might be worn by a North or South Indian bride on her special day will be reviewed here:

- *maangatika/ tika/ tikli,* a pearled or gold chain hooked to the center hair parting with a small or elaborate jewelled pendant that hangs on the brow; this is specifically bridal or classical dancer's jewelry.

- *matha patti/ nethi chutti,* hairline ornament similar to the tika, but with 3 gold chains that support it at the hairline and parting.

- *jhoomka/ jimmikki,* the dangling jewelled earrings, also supported on chains that attach to the hair. Again, this is formal bridal jewelry, often in meenakari (enamelled gold) and bead work. Smaller earrings of this type are not uncommon for regular wear.

- *nath/ mookuthi,* large jeweled gold or silver nose-ring, with dependent chain that attaches to the hair on one side for support. This, along with the wedding sari and tika pendant, were and still are in the Punjab, the traditional gift of the bride's maternal uncle.

- *mangalasutra, or maangalayam,* generally a gold chain necklace, often with additional gold or black beads and/or pendant(s) with caste/subcaste/ community significance, tied around the neck of a bride by the groom during a significant moment in the wedding ceremony. Also called a *tali* or *thali,* it can be a simple gold pendant on several, usually three, tumeric-tinted threads, knotted by auspicious, i.e. married women with living husbands, sumangalis, and then tied with three knots around the neck of the bride by the groom. It fulfils the purpose of a Western wedding ring, and will be put aside and not worn again by a widowed woman.

- *haar,* decorative gold, jeweled necklace in many lengths and designs.

- *baajubandh,* gold or silver jeweled armlet; this item formerly held an amulet.

- *mekhala, kardhani,* waist chain, often silver, with silver key-chain holder.

- *kamarband/ oddiyanam,* gold wedding belt, worn with a sari, lehengha or lengha; more often seen worn with classical dance attire.

- *arsi,* thumb-ring with inset mirror. This carries a heavy weight of romance as it was once the means of the first view a veiled bride had of her new husband, seated beside her at her wedding ceremony.
- *anguti,* a gold ring, worn on the index finger, with or without gemstone.
- *hath panja,* wristlet with five rings attached, decorated with gems and tiny bells.

- *choodamani,* large round gold bejewelled hair ornament fixed at the crown and circled with a wreath of jasmine buds.

- *sooryan chandran,* gold ornamental hair brooches, in the shape of sun and moon, fixed on either side of the hair parting.

- *kankan/ bala/ kada,* decorative thick bangles and cuff bangles in gold or

elaborate kundan work (gems and precious beads set in gold) and/or ornamented in meenakari.

- *churi,* slender gold or colored glass bangle, worn in sets of 12.

- *mama chura,* the red and white ivory bangles worn by a Punjabi bride, presented by her maternal uncle; they are placed on her arms, up to four dozen, in a special ceremony, with silver and beaten gold ornaments (*kaleeras*) attached at the wrist.

- *nupur/ payal,* anklet, usually a silver chain or cuff and chains with tiny bells; sometimes with one to five toe rings attached. Gold anklets are not common as silver has been preferred for a lowly body part such as the foot.

- *bichwa/ amvat/ nupur,* also, silver toe-rings, traditionally two simple silver bands.

- *jhoomar,* silver or gold hair ornament with spreading chains.

- *parandi/ kunjalam/ pinnal,* beaded, silk ornament for the end of a braid.

Some family traditions do include the ceremony in which the bridegroom fixes silver rings on the toes (usually the second toe of both feet) of the bride as an essential step in the later part of the main ceremony. It was a widely recognized sign of her new wifely status. Modern young women have hesitated in recent decades to include this tradition and have tended not to wear toe rings. But, like multiple ear piercings and nose-studs, they are now part of a fashion trend that comes and goes, and even vary in design.

Folklore attributes the use of toe rings or anklets to none other than Sita in the Ramayana. Rama's brother is asked if he recognizes the jewelry which Sita had dropped unnoticed by Ravana as she was being abducted at great speed. In a hyperbole of modesty, Lakshmana simply replies that the only jewelry he does recognize are her anklets which he sees as he prostrates in front of his elder brother's wife seeking her blessings!

This episode is included in P. Lal's prose transcreation of the Ramayana (Lal, P. *The Ramayana of Valmiki* , p. 89, 1989) citing Kishkindha, 6-22:

ऐवं उक्तः तु रामेण लक्श्मणो वाक्यमिदमब्रवीत्
नाहम् जानामि केयूरे नाहम् जानामि कुन्डले
नूपुरेतु अभिजानामि नित्यम् पाद अभिवन्दनात्

ēvam ukta: tu raamēṇa lakshmaṇō vākyamidamabravīt
naaham jānāmi kēyūrē nāham jānāmi kuṇḍalē
nūpurētu abhijānāmi nityam pāda abhivandanāt

Upon hearing Rama, Lakshmana responded thus: I cannot recognize her bracelets, nor her earrings but I do recognize her anklets on her feet as I see them while prostrating in front of her (to seek her blessings)

Addenda:

There are distinct regional ornaments worn nowadays mainly by brides. Besides the Punjabi mama chura, these include the Kashmiri cord earring extensions, iron bangles (loha) and silver filigree in eastern India, and red lac bangles, and pearl strings in Maharashtra. Designs range from geometric to natural motifs of flowers, leaves, seeds, bird, serpentine, butterfly and animal shapes. While gold has always been the preferred metal and diamond the preferred gemstone, jewelry in India has generally been made of many substances: silver and other metals and auspicious metallic combinations such as panchalohana; wood and bamboo; lac; glass and ceramic.

Historically Indian men have not been backward in adorning themselves in ropes of pearls, gold chains, armlets and cuffs, and jewelled rings. The modern groom is more likely to sport a good watch and possibly a gold ring with a lucky gemstone. If he has chosen to wear a turban, he might also add such turban ornaments as such as the *sarpech* or jewelled aigret brooch fastened to the front, or a gold chain set (*kalagi*) for draping over the turban.

2. Indian Bridal Clothing.

Western guests at a Hindu wedding are likely to marvel at the rainbow river of silks visible in the ranks of the guests alone. What could a bride wear to stand out in this riot of color? Generally not white, although a richly gold-embroidered red or green bordered white or ivory-colored saree is often worn in the south of India.

Traditionally, the color for Indian brides has always been a shade of red or gold. Nowadays fashion dictates what shade and what decoration. The current trend is for heavily beaded, gold and/or silver embroidered attire which can range from saree and blouse to skirt, blouse and veil or tunic, pant and veil combinations from one part or day of the celebration to the finale.

Clothing for the bride includes:

- *ghomta/ odhani,* veil or shawl in varying lengths and drapes; there are many more regional names for this item; in the Rig Veda, Suryaa's shawl is the only bridal garment that is defined with any clarity as she is otherwise clothed in metaphors and it remains, in North India, the quintessential garment that is or used to be draped over whatever else the bride was wearing, be it saree or skirt or salwar kameez. In Vedic times it was gifted after the wedding to the officiating priest. In historic times it was one of the gifts of the maternal uncle to the bride. It was generally red, trimmed with gold lace or tinsel ribbon. More often now it is integrated into the total outfit.

- *anchal,* skirt, with an attached or extended wraparound veil or shawl, worn with a choli; the loose end of the saree or veil.

- *choli,* short, close-fitting blouse, traditionally with short sleeves, otherwise elbow-length or sleeveless; worn under sarees and with skirt outfits.

- *sari/ saree,* draped garment of usually 6 (sometimes 9) yards of silk or silk interwoven with gold thread, usually in shades of red or gold for weddings, with a gold thread border or embroidery.

- *salwar kameez,* in red velvet or silk; this is the two piece outfit of the Punjabi bride: tunic, matching pants gathered at the ankle, with added veil or shawl (*dupatta*), all gold and bead embroidery, and edged with gold lace.

- *lehnga/ lehenga* outfit, ankle-length paneled skirt, with matching choli and veil; a heavily embroidered, bejwelled version is now a wedding favorite. It can also be worn with a kameez or sleeved tunic. The traditional Rajasthani *ghagara* is a many pleated or gathered, almost circular, skirt, worn with choli and veil.

- *garara/ gagra* outfit, as above except with a divided skirt or pant effect from waist to knee, flouncing out from knee to ankle, worn with tunic top and veil.

Clothing for the groom:
The modern mid twentieth century urban Indian groom was inclined to turn up in a Western-style suit, topped with a turban or decorated white pith and tinsel coronet, further decorated with a small veil of jasmine bud strings. But just as weddings in India have become more elaborate in the past few decades and a complete bridal industry has sprung forth to meet the need, so has the idea of attire for the groom evolved. Unlike in the West, the role of groom is not eclipsed by the role of the bride. He shares an equal footing, a procession of his own, and a larger speaking role. His clothes are still less elaborate in color and style but can be equally elegant. While a suit may still be preferred for a wedding reception, some of the following garments for the main event:

-*dhoti/ antariya/ lungi,* a 6-yard length of fine cotton or silk, white or natural, unstitched, draped from the waist to the ankle and tied in front; often passed through the legs for a pant effect, with one end hanging in folds at the front. This garment can have a simple gold or elaborate colored silk and gold woven border. Worn with an upper

cloth, this is still the wedding garment of choice for South Indian brahmins.
- *uttariya,* upper cloth, usually worn with a dhoti, across the bare upper body, or as a waist band, or over the shoulder with a kurta or jacket.
- *kayabandhan,* waist cloth, for tying or wrapping.
- *sherwani* outfit, a tunic-style coat or long shirt, differing in length, worn over a dhoti, drawstring straight pants or churidhar pants. Worn long in embroidered heavy silk with matching pants or churidhars, with or without a matching vest or kamarband, this is the favorite current wedding attire for the average groom.
- *churidhar,* origin of the pants style known as jodhpurs in the West; silk or cotton pants tight from the knee down.

- *achkan,* a fitted jacket, better known as a Nehru jacket in the West, with high collar, long sleeve, in light wool, heavy silk or cotton; for a wedding this jacket can be in white, ivory, natural, brown, or light pastels; with gold brocade or embroidered detail.
- *kamarband/ patka,* the groom's waist band is usually brocaded silk.
- *sadri/* vest, vest or waistcoat in embroidered light wool or silk brocade.

- *pagari/ safa/ turban,* fitted headgear or a long unstitched length of cloth, usually fine cotton, wound around a cap or coiled hair. This is a historical hallmark of Indian men's attire, and at one time each Indian state had its distinct style in terms of color, fabric, pattern and method of tying. For weddings, it is worn in bright cotton or rich silk brocade. Some grooms do not cover their heads at all, and some traditions call for small coronets or caps in varying styles.

- *jootis/ mojaris,* leather shoes with pointed toes made of leather in camel, goat or sheepskin; first described for the West by Alexander's historians, these are a traditional favorite for wedding wear, especially at their finest, worked with gold embroidery and beads.

3. Floral adornments:

Flowers probably preceded jewelry as ornaments for the bride in ancient India. They are still an important part of the ceremony. Aside from the flowers used to bedeck the mantap, and petals used to sprinkle on the bride, flower accessories include:

- *malas,* wedding garlands for bride and groom to exchange with each other at a signal part of the ceremony, Jai Mala; and for other members of the wedding party to exchange, if desired, at the time of Milni or Swagat(am).
- *malli poo,* jasmine buds roped around the full chignon (*juda*) or small side chignon in the case of some South Indian brides.
- *kondai,* jasmine, and other flowers mounted onto stiff paper, cane or cloth to construct floral coronets or the long *moggina jade* that covers the braid of a Mysore bride.

- headpiece or coronet, of the Bengali bride and groom, crafted of white pith.

- jasmine bud "veil" screen for a North Indian bridegroom: short vertical strings attached to the front of the turban or coronet.

4. Indian Bridal Cosmetics.

- *sindur or sindoor,* the red vermillion powder or paste that is another hall mark of the traditional bride when applied to the simanta, the parting of her hair, during the wedding ceremony. It is also used for the bindu.

- *bindu, tilaka,* the round mark or streak on the forehead of the bride which used to denote a married woman. The bindu is now a fashion trend, varied by color, shape and substance. Jewels, beads and sequins have been popular more recently for brides and for general wear. It has also been a fashion not to wear it at all, except for weddings, pujas and special events. A black dot, made with kohl or a modern eyebrow pencil is sometimes applied somewhere on the bride's face to ward off the evil eye.

- *alaktak,* bright red foot paint, seen mainly now on the soles and edges of feet of classical Indian dancers, has largely been supplanted by the use of mehndi or henna.

- *mehndi,* a paste made from the dried leaves of the henna plant is used for elaborate tattoo-like decorations on hands and feet in a delicate shade of reddish brown. The patterns last for around three weeks, and the application process for the bride and her wedding party is now a popular pre-wedding event.

- *haldi,* turmeric; the yellow powder made from the root of this plant was an important part of beauty preparations for the bride-to-be. After the pre-wedding ritual bathing, turmeric was rubbed into her skin to give her a much admired golden glow. Turmeric still has a ritual use during weddings as well as other Hindu rites. It is applied to color the coconut for Kanyadanam and to tint the rice (*akshata*) used for blessings.

- *kohl/ kajal/ anjana,* sulfide of antimony used for lining for the eyes; usually in powder form or made from carbon and herbs mixed into a paste. Nowadays it is usually replaced by modern makeup.

- *sandal* paste, from the naturally aromatic roots and heartwood of the sandalwood tree (Latin s*antalum album*), used to create the line of white dots that follow the twin arches of the eyebrows and accentuate this recognized item of beauty as well as the bindu for Bengali and other North Indian brides. Nowadays this is also sometimes replaced by a line of colored designs, either painted, natural leaf or petal, or sequins or jewels.

It is important to keep in mind that terminology for clothing and jewelry differs from one end of India to the other, expressed in many languages and traditions. Only the most common terms are included here.

Appendix VII: Pujas

Note that the materials and other ritual arrangements used at the pujas may be brought to the mantap later for use during the processionals and the main ceremony. Abbreviated pujas to Mahaganapati and Gowri are included below:

Preparation of the altar:

First and foremost begin with cleansing, i.e. clean the area where the altar is to be set up. This should face the eastern direction if possible. A small bench or a wooden table or a cardboard box covering an area no larger than 36" x 24" and about 15" to 24" tall is adequate. Cover it with a clean cloth and arrange a picture of the god/goddess to be worshipped. Similarly pictures or images of the family godhead and guru may also be arranged on the altar.

Materials and arrangement:

• Prepare one or two deepas (lamps) with cotton wicks soaking in oil. Place the lamp/s about 6" in front of the picture if it is one lamp, or about 10" apart if two lamps. Do not light these until you are ready to begin the puja.
• Prepare a worship plate (stainless steel, silver or other metal, 12" to 24" diameter) by placing on it small vessels (cup-like, preferably metallic) of kumkum, turmeric, one square of camphor, sandal powder or paste, a dozen agarbatti sticks (incense sticks), a bell, and a matchbox.
• Prepare another plate, 12" or 24" diameter, metallic or wicker and put a variety or five kinds of fruits (bananas, apples, oranges, etc.) and a variety of leaves and flowers.
• You will need an arati plate. This can be a small metal plate with one or five wicks soaking in oil or ghee.

You will also need a small cup of akshata (raw rice dampened slightly with water and colored with turmeric.) This mixture should be prepared a day earlier so that it is completely dry.

• Covered dishes of your favorite prasaadam or sweets may be placed in front of the altar.

• A metallic urn large enough to contain a couple of mugs of water should be filled with water and placed in front of the altar. You will need a smaller vessel, preferably a metallic straightwalled tumbler into which water will be poured during the service.

• A dispenser, called uddharana, or a simple metallic spoon to dispense water from the tumbler will be needed.

• You will need a piece of cloth, white for a male deity and colorful cloth for a goddess for an offering during the puja.

Now you are ready to begin. Light the lamps and a couple of agarbattis. In a few moments you will be invoking and receiving a godhead and therefore the principal mood should be one of joy and bhakti, but the mind should be relaxed.

PUJA TO MAHAGANAPATI

It is customary for the bridegroom to perform, with his family and friends attending, a puja to Mahaganapati and to pray for a successful wedding ceremony without any vighna or obstacle.

After ringing the bell to ward off any bad vibrations and tendencies in the area and before starting the puja proper, it is essential to contemplate Mahaganapati to assure ourselves that no obstacles interfere with a smooth performance of the puja rituals. Thus, with folded hands chant the following:

करिश्यमाणस्य कर्मणः निर्विघ्नेन परिसमाप्त्यर्थं
आदौ महागणपति स्मरणं करिश्ये
kariśyamāṇasya karmaṇa: nirvighnēna parisamāptyartham
ādau mahāgaṇapati smaraṇam karishyē

So that the ceremonies we are about to undertake proceed to completion without any obstacles we meditate on Mahaganapati.

Similarly the grhadevata, i.e. the family godhead, who is ever present bestowing protection to the family at all times is now invoked. Chant as follows:

गृह देवतां ध्यायामि
ध्यानं समर्पयामि
gr̥ha dēvatām dhyāyāmi
dhyānam samarpayāmi

I respectfully contemplate our family Godhead.

Finally, it is necessary to pay respect to the family guru (guru here refers to aachaaryaas such as Adi Shankarachaarya, Ramanujaachaarya, Madhvaachaarya or others) and offer prayer before beginning the ceremony by chanting:

गुरु ब्रह्मा गुरुर्विष्णुः गुरुर्देवो म्उहगव्µउरउ
गुरु साक्षात् परब्रह्म तस्मै श्रीगुरुवे नमः

guru brahmā gururviṣṇu: gururdēvō mahēśwara:
guru sākṣāt parabrahma tasmai śrīguruvē nama:

Salutations to the preceptor who is verily Brahma, Vishnu and Maheshwara and who personifies the Supreme Being

Shuddhi (Cleansing)

In order to assure ourselves that any and all evil tendencies are removed from the worship room, we start with a prayer to Shiva whose very invocation is believed to clear out any troubling vibrations:

ऒं नमः प्रणवार्थाय शुद्ध ज्नानैक मूर्तये
निर्मलाय प्रशांताय दक्षिणा मूर्तये नमः
ōm nama: praṇavārthāya śuddha jnānaika mūrtayē
nirmalāya praśāntāya dakṣiṇā mūrtayē nama:

I salute the Lord of the Southern direction who is the very embodiment of the sacred symbol Om and of pure knowledge and eternal peace.

Next we need to invoke and invite the sacred rivers to fill the metallic vessel. This water is used to cleanse and offer throughout the worship. Start pouring water from one vessel into the smaller one as you chant:

गंगेच यमुनेचैव गोदावरी सरस्वति
नर्मदा सिंधु कावेरी जलेःस्मिन् सन्निधिं कुरु
gangēcha yamunēchaiva gōdāvarī saraswati
narmadā sindhu kāvērī jalē:smin sannidhim kuru

O Ganga, Yamuna, Godavari, Saraswati, Narmada,
Sindhu and Kaveri waters, please be present in this place.

Now that we have received the sacred waters, it is time to symbolically cleanse our hands by offering a spoonful (uddharane) of water into the hands of the principals (bridegroom, his parents) by wiping the hands with reverence as we chant:

अपवित्रः पवित्रोवा सर्वावस्थां गतोपिवा
यःस्मरेत् पुंडरीकाक्षं बाह्याभ्यंतरः शुचिः
apavitra: pavitrōvā sarvāvasthām gatōpivā
ya:smarēt pundarīkākṣam bāhyābhyantara: śuci:

May anything unholy be made holy, may all lower tendencies depart,
cleansing both inside and out, as we remember Pundareekaaksha.

Prayer

वक्रतुंड महाकाय सूर्यकोटि समप्रभा
निर्विघ्नं कुरु मेदेव सर्व कार्येशु सर्वदा
vakratunda mahākāya sōryakōti samaprabhā
nirvighnam kuru mēdēva sarva kāryēśu sarvadā

My Lord with curved tusk, immense body, and whose brilliance
matches that of a million suns, please remove all obstacles
in all my undertakings at all times.

Upacharas (Puja offerings)

Now we are ready to invoke Ganapati and offer Upacharas (reception with reverence). With folded hands focus on the picture of the deity as you chant the following:

ऒं श्रीमन्महागणाधिपतयेनमः
ōm śrīmanmahāgaṇādhipatayēnama:

I offer my salutations to Mahaganapati.

Now offer a few grains of akshata with your right hand such that the grains fall on the picture gently as you chant:

ऒं श्रीमन्महागणाधिपतयेनमः
ōm śrīmanmahāgaṇādhipatayēnama:
आवाहनं समर्पयामि
āvāhanam samarpayāmi

I offer an invocation to you.

Offer akshata as before such that the grains fall on the altar as you chant:

ऒं श्रीमन्महागणाधिपतयेनमः
ōm śrīmanmahāgaṇādhipatayēnama:
आसनं समर्पयामि
āsanam samarpayāmi

I offer a seat for you.

Offer an uddharana full of water at the feet of the deity chanting:

ऑं श्रीमन्महागणाधिपतयेनमः

ōm śrīmanmahāgaṇādhipatayēnama:

पाद्यं समर्पयामि

pādyam samarpayāmi

I offer water to your feet.

Offer an uddharana full of water to the hands of the deity chanting:

ऑं श्रीमन्महागणाधिपतयेनमः

ōm śrīmanmahāgaṇādhipatayēnama:

अर्घ्यं समर्पयामि

arghyam samarpayāmi

I offer water to your hands.

Offer an uddharana full of water to the hands of the deity as you chant:

ऑं श्रीमन्महागणाधिपतयेनमः

ōm śrīmanmahāgaṇādhipatayēnama:

आचमनीयं समर्पयामि

ācamanīyam samarpayāmi

I offer water to quench thirst.

Offer some sweet drink (fruit juice or honey) as you chant:

ऑं श्रीमन्महागणाधिपतयेनमः

ōm śrīmanmahāgaṇādhipatayēnama:

मधुपर्कं समर्पयामि

madhuparkam samarpayāmi

I offer some sweet drink.

Symbolically offer water to bathe or pour water over the deity to bathe as you chant:

ओं श्रीमन्महागणाधिपतयेनमः

ōm śrīmanmahāgaṇādhipatayēnama

शुद्धोदकस्नानं समर्पयामि

śuddhōdakasnānam samarpayāmi

I offer clean water to bathe.

Offer again an uddharana full of water to the hands of the deity or picture as you chant:

ओं श्रीमन्महागणाधिपतयेनमः

ōm śrīmanmahāgaṇādhipatayēnama:

स्नानानंतरं आचमनीयं समर्पयामि

snānānantaram ācamanīyam samarpayāmi

I offer water to drink after the bath.

Symbolically offer a clean piece of cloth to represent gifts of clothing:

ओं श्रीमन्महागणाधिपतयेनमः

ōm śrīmanmahāgaṇādhipatayēnama:

वस्त्रान् समर्पयामि

vastrān samarpayāmi

I offer clothing.

Symbolically offer a clean piece of string to represent a new yagnopaveet:

ओं श्रीमन्महागणाधिपतयेनमः

ōm śrīmanmahāgaṇādhipatayēnama:

उपवीतं समर्पयामि

upavītam samarpayāmi

I offer a new yagnopaveet.

Apply to the forehead some sandal paste:

ओं श्रीमन्महागणाधिपतयेनमः

ōm śrīmanmahāgaṇādhipatayēnama:

गंधान् धारयामि

gandhān dhārayāmi

I offer sandal paste.

Offer some akshata:

ओं श्रीमन्महागणाधिपतयेनमः

ōm śrīmanmahāgaṇādhipatayēnama:

अक्शतान् समर्पयामि

akṣatān samarpayāmi

I offer akshata.

Offer flowers or petals of flowers to the picture or the deity:

ओं श्रीमन्महागणाधिपतयेनमः

ōm śrīmanmahāgaṇādhipatayēnama:
पुष्पाणि समर्पयामि
puṣpāṇi samarpayāmi

I offer flowers in worship.

With folded hands chant the several names of Mahaganapati:

ओं सुमुखाय नमः ऐकदंताय नमः कपिलाय नमः गजकर्णकाय नमः
लंबोदराय नमः विकटाय नमः विघ्नराजाय नमः विनायकाय नमः
धूम्रकेतवे नमः गणाधिपाय नमः फालचंद्राय नमः गजाननाय नमः
वक्रतुंडाय नमः शूर्पकर्णाय नमः हेरंबाय नमः स्कंद पूर्वजाय नमः

ōm sumukhāya nama: ēkadantāya nama: kapilāya nama:
gajakarṇakāya nama: lambōdarāya nama: vikaṭāya nama:
vighnarājāya nama: vināyakāya nama: dhōmrakētavē nama:
gaṇādhipāya nama: phālacandrāya nama: gajānanāya nama:
vakratuṇḍāya nama: śūrpakarṇāya nama: hērambāya nama:
skanda pūrvajāya nama:

I salute that Lord who has a beautiful face, single tusk, red color, elephant ears, large belly and who is a source of happiness, ruler of obstacles, supreme, fire-like in stature, head of the army, with crescent moon for crest, face of an elephant, curved tusk, sharp-eared, powerful, the elder brother of Skanda.

ओं श्रीमन्महागणाधिपतयेनमः
ōm śrīmanmahāgaṇādhipatayēnama:

Offer incense by fanning incense smoke with your right hand towards the altar:

धूपं आघ्रापयामि

dhūpam āghrāpayāmi

I offer fragrance in worship.

Lift the lamp and show it to the picture or deity such that it illuminates the face:

ऒं श्रीमन्महागणाधिपतयेनमः

ōm śrīmanmahāgaṇādhipatayēnama:

दीपं दर्शयामि

dīpam darśayāmi

I offer sacred light.

Lift the plate of fruits, leaves and flowers in reverence and offer them:

ऒं श्रीमन्महागणाधिपतयेनमः

ōm śrīmanmahāgaṇādhipatayēnama:

नानाविध परिमळ पत्र फल पुश्पाणि समर्पयामि

nānāvidha parimaḷa patra phala puṣpāṇi samarpayāmi

I offer a variety of flowers, leaves and fruits.

Now lift the cover off the sweets/prasaadam and offer it as you chant:

ऒं श्रीमन्महागणाधिपतयेनमः

ōm śrīmanmahāgaṇādhipatayēnama:
नैवेद्यं निवेदयामि
naivēdyam nivēdayāmi

I offer delicious food to you.

Sprinkle a few drops of water with the uddharana on the food as you chant:
प्राणाय स्वाहा, अपानाय स्वाहा, व्यानाय स्वाहा,
उदानाय स्वाहा, समानाय स्वाहा, ब्रह्मणे स्वाहा
prāṇāya swāhā, apānāya swāhā, vyānāya swāhā,
udānāya swāhā, samānāya swāhā, brahmaṇē swāhā

These are invocations and hails to the various wind elements in our body which promote digestion. The final hail is to the creator Brahma. Continue to offer water as you chant:

ओं श्रीमन्महागणाधिपतयेनमः
ōm śrīmanmahāgaṇādhipatayēnama:
मध्ये मध्ये आचमनीयं समर्पयामि
madhyē madhyē ācamanīyam samarpayāmi

I offer more water as you partake of the offering.

Offer a coin as you chant:
ओं श्रीमन्महागणाधिपतयेनमः
ōm śrīmanmahāgaṇādhipatayēnama:
सुवर्ण पुश्पं समर्पयामि
suvarṇa pushpam samarpayāmi

I offer gold to you.

This completes the Upacharas.

Pradakshina

Now stand up and do a pradakshina (circumambulation) turning three times to your right.

ओं श्रीमन्महागणाधिपतयेनमः

ōm śrīmanmahāgaṇādhipatayēnama:

यानिकानिच पापानि जन्मांतर कृतानि च

तानि तानि विनश्यंति प्रदक्षिणं पदे पदे

yānikānica pāpāni janmāntara kr̥tāni ca
tāni tāni vinaśyanti pradakṣiṇam padē padē

Whatever sins I have committed in all my lives,
May all be absolved as I circumambulate in worship of you

Conclusion

Now the Puja can be completed with an aarati. *Om jayajagadishahare* is recommended. If the ashtoththara (108 names) is to be chanted then the aarati follows that. After the aarati is complete, take the aarati plate around so that the devotees can receive the blessing by reverentially cupping their hands downwards to receive the warmth of the flame and touching their eyes with the cupped hands.

We conclude the puja ceremony by chanting the following two shlokas.

त्वमॆव माताच पिता त्वमॆव
त्वमॆव बंधुश्च सखा त्वमॆव
त्वमॆव विद्या द्रविणम् त्वमॆव
त्वमॆव सर्वं मम दॆव दॆव

tvamēva mātāca pitā tvamēva
tvamēva bandhuśca sakhā tvamēva
tvamēva vidyā draviṇam tvamēva
tvamēva sarvam mama dēva dēva

You alone are our mother and father
You alone are our sibling and friend
You alone are our knowledge and prosperity
You alone are everything to us
My Lord, my Lord

कायॆन वाचा मनसॆंन्द्रियैर्वा
बुध्यात्मनावा प्रकृतॆ स्वभावात्
करॊमि यद्यत् सकलं परस्मै
नारायणायॆति समर्पयामि

kāyēna vācā manasēnndriyairvā
budhyātmanāvā prakr̥tē swabhāvāt
karōmi yadyat sakalam parasmai
nārāyaṇāyēti samarpayāmi

Whatever I have performed through my action,
speech, thought, knowledge, or my natural habit,

may all that be surrendered to Srimannarayana.

The prasaad (consecrated food) may now be distributed and enjoyed after the Shanti Mantra (Peace) chant:

ओं सहना ववतु
सहनौ भुनक्तु
सहवीर्यं करवावहै
तेजस्विना वधीतमस्तु
मा विद् विशा वहै
ओं शान्तिः, शान्तिः, शान्तिः

ōm sahanā vavatu
sahanau bhunaktu
sahavīryam karavāvahai
tejaswinā vadhītamastu
mā vid vishā vahai
ōm śānti: śānti: śānti:

May Brahman protect us
may we dine together
let us work together with great energy
let us be illumined together
let us live in harmony
peace, peace, peace!

□□□□□□

PUJA TO GAURI BY THE BRIDE

Materials and arrangement: All the preliminaries required for Gauri Puja are identical to those shown above for the Puja to Mahaganapati. Changes begin from the section designated as Prayer and continue as shown below. Also note in the list of materials, a set of ornaments such as necklace, bangles etc., relevant as offering to a goddess replace the yagnopavitam listed in the Ganapati Puja.

Prayer

सर्व मंगळ मांगल्ये शिवे सर्वार्थ साधिके
शरण्ये त्र्यंबके देवी नारायणी नमोस्तुते
sarva mangaḷa māngalyē śivē sarvārtha sādhikē
śaraṇyē tryambakē dēvī nārāyaṇī namōstutē

O Naaraayani, embodiment of prosperity, personification
of the Shiva aspect, accomplished, protector,
Mother of the Three Worlds, and known as Gauri.

Upacharas

Now we are ready to invoke Gauri and offer Upachaaraas (reception with reverence). With folded hands focus on the picture of the deity as you chant the following:

ओं नमो भगवत्यै सकल देवता शक्तात्मिकायै श्री गौर्यै नमः
ōm namō bhagavatyai sakala dēvatā śaktātmikāyai śrī gauryai nama:

Salutations to Sri Gauri that goddess who personifies
the strengths of all godheads in herself.

Now offer a few grains of akshata with your right hand such that the grains fall on the picture gently as you chant:

ओं नमो भगवत्यै सकल देवता शक्तात्मिकायै श्री गौर्यै नमः
ōm namō bhagavatyai sakala dēvatā śaktātmikāyai śrī gauryai nama:
Salutations to Sri Gauri that goddess who personifies
the strengths of all godheads in herself
आवाहनं समर्पयामि
āvāhanam samarpayāmi

I offer an invocation to you.

Offer akshata as before such that the grains fall on the altar as you chant:

ओं नमो भगवत्यै सकल देवता शक्तात्मिकायै श्री गौर्यै नमः
ōm namō bhagavatyai sakala dēvatā śaktātmikāyai śrī gauryai nama:
Salutations to Sri Gauri that goddess who personifies
the strengths of all godheads in herself.
आसनं समर्पयामि
āsanam samarpayāmi

I offer a seat for you.

Offer an uddharana full of water at the feet of the deity or picture as you chant:
ओं नमो भगवत्यै सकल देवता शक्तात्मिकायै श्री गौर्यै नमः

ōm namō bhagavatyai sakala dēvatā śaktātmikāyai śrī gauryai nama:
Salutations to Sri Gauri that goddess who personifies
the strengths of all godheads in herself
पाद्यं समर्पयामि
pādyam samarpayāmi

I offer water to your feet.

Offer an uddharana full of water to the hands of the deity or picture as you chant:

ओं नमो भगवत्यै सकल देवता शक्तात्मिकायै श्री गौर्यै नमः
ōm namō bhagavatyai sakala dēvatā śaktātmikāyai śrī gauryai nama:
Salutations to Sri Gauri that goddess who personifies
the strengths of all godheads in herself.
अर्घ्यं समर्पयामि
arghyam samarpayāmi

I offer water to your hands.

Offer again an uddharana full of water to the hands of the deity or picture as you chant:

ओं नमो भगवत्यै सकल देवता शक्तात्मिकायै श्री गौर्यै नमः
ōm namō bhagavatyai sakala dēvatā śaktātmikāyai śrī gauryai nama:
Salutations to Sri Gauri that goddess who personifies
the strengths of all godheads in herself.
आचमनीयं समर्पयामि
ācamanīyam samarpayāmi

I offer water to quench thirst.

Offer some sweet drink (fruit juice or honey) as you chant:

ओं नमो भगवत्यै सकल देवता शक्तात्मिकायै श्री गौर्यै नमः

ōm namō bhagavatyai sakala dēvatā śaktātmikāyai śrī gauryai nama:

Salutations to Sri Gauri that goddess who personifies
the strengths of all godheads in herself.

मधुपर्कं समर्पयामि

madhuparkam samarpayāmi

I offer a sweet drink.

Symbolically offer water to bathe or pour water over the deity to bathe as you chant:

ओं नमो भगवत्यै सकल देवता शक्तात्मिकायै श्री गौर्यै नमः

ōm namō bhagavatyai sakala dēvatā śaktātmikāyai śrī gauryai nama:

Salutations to Sri Gauri that goddess who personifies
the strengths of all godheads in herself.

शुद्धोदकस्नानं समर्पयामि

śuddhōdakasnānam samarpayāmi

I offer clean water to bathe.

Offer again an uddharana full of water to the hands of the deity or picture as you chant:

ओं नमो भगवत्यै सकल देवता शक्तात्मिकायै श्री गौर्यै नमः

ōm namō bhagavatyai sakala dēvatā śaktātmikāyai śrī gauryai nama:

Salutations to Sri Gauri that goddess who personifies
the strengths of all godheads in herself.

स्नानानंतरं आचमनीयं समर्पयामि

snānānantaram ācamanīyam samarpayāmi

I offer water to drink after the bath.

Symbolically offer a clean piece of cloth to represent gifts of clothing:

ओं नमो भगवत्यै सकल देवता शक्तात्मिकायै श्री गौर्यै नमः

ōm namō bhagavatyai sakala dēvatā śaktātmikāyai śrī gauryai nama:

Salutations to Sri Gauri that goddess who personifies the strengths of all godheads in herself.

वस्त्रान् समर्पयामि

vastrān samarpayāmi

I offer clothing.

Symbolically offer ornaments as you chant:

ओं नमो भगवत्यै सकल देवता शक्तात्मिकायै श्री गौर्यै नमः

ōm namō bhagavatyai sakala dēvatā śaktātmikāyai śrī gauryai nama:

Salutations to Sri Gauri that goddess who personifies the strengths of all godheads in herself.

सकलाभरणानि समर्पयामि

sakalābharaṇāni samarpayāmi

I offer all ornaments.

Apply to the forehead some sandal paste:

ओं नमो भगवत्यै सकल देवता शक्तात्मिकायै श्री गौर्यै नमः

ōm namō bhagavatyai sakala dēvatā śaktātmikāyai śrī gauryai nama:

Salutations to Sri Gauri that goddess who personifies
the strengths of all godheads in herself.

गंधान् धारयामि

gandhān dhārayāmi

I offer sandal paste.

Offer some akshata:

ओं नमो भगवत्यै सकल देवता शक्तात्मिकायै श्री गौर्यै नमः

ōm namō bhagavatyai sakala dēvatā śaktātmikāyai śrī gauryai nama:

Salutations to Sri Gauri that goddess who personifies
the strengths of all godheads in herself.

अक्शतान् समर्पयामि

akśatān samarpayāmi

I offer akshata.

Offer flowers or petals of flowers to the picture or the deity:

ओं नमो भगवत्यै सकल देवता शक्तात्मिकायै श्री गौर्यै नमः

ōm namō bhagavatyai sakala dēvatā śaktātmikāyai śrī gauryai nama:

Salutations to Sri Gauri that goddess who personifies
the strengths of all godheads in herself.

पुष्पाणि समर्पयामि

puṣpāṇi samarpayāmi

I offer flowers in worship.

With folded hands chant the several names of Gauri:

ओं श्री गणेश जनन्यै नमः ओं स्वर्ण गौर्यै नमः ओं शंकर्यै नमः
ओं मांगल्य दायिन्यै नमः ओं सर्वकाल सुमंगल्यै नमः ओं त्रिपुरसौंदर्यै नमः
ओं रूप सौभाग्यै नमः ओं परमानंद दायै नमः ओं आद्यंत रहितायै नमः
ओं महामात्रे नमः ओं स्उव्उगत्µउय्उगत नमः ओं म्उहगव्µउय्उगत नमः
ओं दीनरक्शिण्यै नमः ओं पापनाशिन्यै नमः ओं जगन्मात्रे नमः ओं कृपापूर्णायै नमः
ओं श्री गौरीमातायै नमः

ōm śrī gaṇēśa jananyai nama: ōm svarṇa gauryai nama:
ōm śankaryai nama: ōm māngalya dāyinyai nama:
ōm sarvakāla sumangalyai nama: ōm tripurasaundaryai nama:
ōm rūpa saubhāgyai nama: ōm paramānanda dāyai nama:
ōm ādyanta rahitāyai nama: ōm mahāmātrē nama:
ōm sarvaiśvaryai nama: ōm mahēśvaryai nama:
ōm dīnarakṣiṇyai nama: ōm pāpanāśinyai nama:
ōm jaganmātrē nama: ōm kūpāpūrṇāyai nama:
ōm śrī gaurīmātāyai nama:

Salutations to the mother of Ganesha, Golden Gauri, consort of Sankara,
bestower of the mangalya, one who is good fortune forever, beauty of the
Three Worlds, rich in beauty, bestower of bliss, one who is free of
beginning and end, Great Mother, possessor of all wealth,
consort of Maheswara, protector of the poor, destroyer of sins,
mother of the universe, full of compassion,
Om Salutations to Mother Gauri!

ओं नमो भगवत्यै सकल देवता शक्तात्मिकायै श्री गौर्यै नमः

ōm namō bhagavatyai sakala dēvatā śaktātmikāyai śrī gauryai nama:

Salutations to Sri Gauri that goddess who personifies
the strengths of all godheads in herself.

Offer incense by motioning incense smoke with your right hand towards the altar:

धूपं आघ्रापयामि

dhūpam āghrāpayāmi

I offer fragrance in worship.

Lift the lamp and show it to the picture or deity such that it illuminates the face:

ओं नमो भगवत्यै सकल देवता शक्तात्मिकायै श्री गौर्यै नमः

ōm namō bhagavatyai sakala dēvatā śaktātmikāyai śrī gauryai nama:

Salutations to Sri Gauri that goddess who personifies
the strengths of all godheads in herself.

दीपं दर्शयामि

dīpam darśayāmi

I offer sacred light.

Lift the plate of fruits, leaves and flowers in reverence and offer them:

ओं नमो भगवत्यै सकल देवता शक्तात्मिकायै श्री गौर्यै नमः

ōm namō bhagavatyai sakala dēvatā śaktātmikāyai śrī gauryai nama:

Salutations to Sri Gauri that goddess who personifies

the strengths of all godheads in herself.
नानाविध परिमळ पत्र फल पुश्पाणि समर्पयामि
nānāvidha parimaḷa patra phala pushpāṇi samarpayāmi

I offer a variety of flowers, leaves and fruits.

Now lift the cover off the sweets/prasaadam and offer it as you chant:

ओं नमो भगवत्यै सकल देवता शक्तात्मिकायै श्री गौर्यै नमः
ōm namō bhagavatyai sakala dēvatā śaktātmikāyai śrī gauryai nama:
Salutations to Sri Gauri that goddess who personifies
the strengths of all godheads in herself.
नैवेद्यं निवेदयामि
naivēdya nivēdayāmi

I offer delicious food to you.

Sprinkle a few drops of water with the uddharana on the food as you chant:

प्राणाय स्वाहा, अपानाय स्वाहा, व्यानाय स्वाहा,
उदानाय स्वाहा, समानाय स्वाहा, ब्रह्मणे स्वाहा
prāṇāya swāhā, apānāya swāhā, vyānāya swāhā,
udānāya swāhā, samānāya swāhā, brahmaṇē swāhā

These are invocations and hails to the various wind elements in our body which promote digestion. The final hail is to the creator Brahma.

Continue to offer water as you chant:

ओं नमो भगवत्यै सकल देवता शक्तात्मिकायै श्री गौर्यै नमः

ōm namō bhagavatyai sakala dēvatā śaktātmikāyai śrī gauryai nama:

Salutations to Sri Gauri that goddess who personifies
the strengths of all godheads in herself

मध्ये मध्ये आचमनीयं समर्पयामि

madhyē madhyē ācamanīyam samarpayāmi

I offer more water as you partake of the offering.

Offer a coin as you chant:

ओं नमो भगवत्यै सकल देवता शक्तात्मिकायै श्री गौर्यै नमः

ōm namō bhagavatyai sakala dēvatā śaktātmikāyai śrī gauryai nama:

Salutations to Sri Gauri that goddess who personifies
the strengths of all godheads in herself.

सुवर्ण पुष्प समर्पयामि

suvarṇa puṣpam samarpayāmi

I offer gold to you.

This completes the Upacharas.

Pradakshina

Now stand up and do a pradakshina (circumambulation) three times, turning to your right:

ओं नमो भगवत्यै सकल देवता शक्तात्मिकायै श्री गौर्यै नमः

ōm namō bhagavatyai sakala dēvatā śaktātmikāyai śrī gauryai nama:

Salutations to Sri Gauri that goddess who personifies
the strengths of all godheads in herself.

यानिकानिच पापानि जन्मांतर कृतानि च
तानि तानि विनश्यंति प्रदक्षिणं पदे पदे
yānikānica pāpāni janmāntara kṛtāni ca
tāni tāni vinaśyanti pradakṣiṇam padē padē

Whatever sins I have committed in all my lives,
May all be absolved as I circumambulate in worship of you.

Conclusion

The concluding part of the ceremony is identical to that shown above for Mahaganapati Puja, ending with distribution of prasaad (consecrated food) and the Shanti Mantra.

ABBREVIATIONS

AV	*Atharva Veda*
AGS	*Ashvalayana Grihya Sutra*
H.	*Hindi*
L.	*Latin*
MBh	*Mahabharata (epic)*
MDS	*Manava Dharma Shastra (Laws of Manu)*
ParasGS	*Paraskara Grihya Sutra*
RA	*Ramayana (epic)*
RV	*Rig Veda*
SV	*Sama Veda*
SSSR	*Sartha Shodasha Samkrta Ratnamala*
VS	*Vajaseya Samhita*
YV	*Yajur Veda*

GLOSSARY of NAMES & TERMS

PLEASE NOTE: the term within parentheses below is transliterated for correct pronunciation, where needed, using the conventional diacritical marks for Indic languages. The lead word reflects common usage. (For further terms related to jewelry and clothing, see Appendix VI)

aarati/arati(ārati), ritual in which a plate or thali with a deepa (oil lamp) and other items of ritual purification such as flowers, incense, kumkum and turmeric, are waved at least three times clockwise around a venerated person or object. Sometimes the plate may contain just water with kumkum dissolved in it and a few grains of akshata.

aayana/ayana (āyana), course or journey; refers to the apparent direction of the sun's course through the sky, uttarayana (north) or dakshinayana (south); cited in a sankalpam.

adhika masa (adhika māsa), an extra month added (a consecutive repetition) once every 3 lunar years, to realign with the solar year; Shunya.

adityas (ādityās), the devas or Vedic gods.

agarbatti, incense stick.

Agni, Vedic god of fire; invoked for all domestic rituals, especially a wedding in which he is considered to be the bride's first guardian and chief performer of the rite itself as well as the recipient of offerings.

Agni Pratishtapana (Agni Pratiṣṭhāpana), the setting up of a fire vessel/altar ready for a fire ritual.

akshata (akṣata), rice tinted with turmeric.

amavāsya, new moon.

Anasūya, a pativrata, wife of the sage Atri.

Angāraka, Mars; one of the Navagrahas, the Nine Planets of Vedic astrology.

Arjuna, chief warrior among the Pandava princes (sons of Pandu) and skillful archer, spiritual son of Indra; hero of the epic Mahabharata.

Arundhati darshanam (ārundhati darśanam), a ceremony in which the bride views Arundhati, a star named after the wife of a sage, noted for her fidelity.

Aryaman/Aaryaman (āryaman), rules of conduct, social code, personified in the Rig Veda, as Aaryama.

ashirvadam (āśirvādam), traditional set of blessings on the couple, accompanied by sprinkling of akshata by the priest and family elders.

Ashmarohana (aśmārohana), ceremonial stepping onto a stone by the bride to symbolize stability in marriage.

Ashwins (Aśvins), the Heavenly Twins, connected with the care of animals, agriculture and medicine; Suryā's escort at her bridal.

Atri, a rishi, one of the Seven Sages of the Saptarishi constellation (L. Ursa Major). His wife, Anasuya, is one of the pativratas evoked along with him in the final ashirvadam or blessing of the couple.

baraat (barāt), groom's arrival at the wedding venue on foot, horseback or by automobile, accompanied by his relatives, and usually by musicians.

Bhagavad Gīta, literally Song of God, the discourse given by Krishna to Arjuna on the battlefield of Kurukshetra in the Sanskrit epic Mahabharata; a crystallization of the meaning of dharma, and now accepted as central to Hindu dogma.

Brahma (pronounced ***Bramha)***, the divine creator, whose age is used to mark the time and moment in Vedic rituals. His day covers 1,000 mahāyugas or 4.32 billion solar years. It is divided into Adi Sandhi (1,728,00 solar years), 14 manvantaras, and 14 Sandhi Kālas; during the latter the earth is covered with water. At the end of each life-span of 100 Brahma years, the cosmos dies. Another Brahma comes into being to recreate life and the worlds again.

brahmin (brāhman), one of the four castes, the priestly or scholarly class, learned in the Vedas.

Brihaspati (Bṛhaspati), also called Guru (Jupiter), one of the Navagrahas; the preceptor of the gods.

chaturyuga (caturyuga), the Four Yugas (Kṛta, Treta, Dwāpara, Kali) or world-ages, as a unit, also known as a mahāyuga.

dakshinayana (dakśināyana), see *āyana.*

deepa (dīpa), lamp fuelled by ghee or oil; mainly for ritual use; a small brass, silver or clay deepa with cotton wick which can be placed on an ārati plate, or a larger size with a handle.

dharmapatni, wife-in-dharma, equivalent of the term 'lawfully wedded wife.'

drushti (dṛṣti), ceremony to ward off the "evil eye."

Dhruva darshanam, ceremony in which the bride views Dhruva (Polaris) the North Star, a symbol of stability.

Dwāpara Yuga, second in the yuga cycle, lasting 834,000 (432,000 x 2) solar years.

Ganapati, elephant-headed god, remover of obstacles; the groom and his family usually perform a puja to this deity, also known as Ganesha, before the wedding.

Gandharva, Vishvavasu *(RV)*, guardian of the bride in her first home, before marriage; later a class of heavenly beings.

Gāthā, sacred song, personified in the Rig Veda.

Gauri Pūja, ceremony of worship offered to the Devi, mother of Ganesha by the bride and her family the day before the wedding, for a good outcome for the ceremony and her new life. (Also: ***Gowri***)

ghee (ghī), butter clarified to preserve it; used to fuel lamps (deepas) of all sizes.

gotra (gō tra), spiritual lineage; each Hindu is considered to be the descendant of a sage, three or five of whom are cited in pravara recitals or in formal identification of the individual.

Grihapravesham (Gṛhapraveśam), homecoming ceremony for the bride.

Gṛhasthāshrama, one of the four stages of life for a Hindu, that of the householder, which begins with the wedding rite. The others are Brahmacharya (student life); Vanaprastha (hermit stage or retirement); and Sanyasashrama (renunciation).

haldi, turmeric in powder form, used as a tinting medium for textiles, food and, formerly, complexion; an auspicious yellow gold color.

Harishchandra and Chandramati, an ideal couple of legend, including the Mahabharata, whose names are evoked in the Ashirvadam.

Hasta Milāp, ceremony in which the bride's father joins the right hands of bride and groom.

Havan(a), fire altar.

Hindu, originally a geographical term given by the Persians to the people who lived around and beyond the River Indus; now used to denote an adherent of Hinduism or Sanātana Dharma.

Hinduism, major religion of India, Sanātana Dharma, a set of beliefs derived primarily from the Vedas and related scriptures.

homa, fire ceremony.

Indra, Vedic King of Heaven, wielder of the thunderbolt; regent of the east.

Jai Mala (Jayamāla), ceremony in which the bride first garlands the groom, signifying her choice, and the groom garlands the bride in consent.

Jeeriga/Jeelakarra-bellam (Jīriga/jīlakarra-bellam), regional custom (Karnataka; Andhra Pradesh), in which the couple offer each other a mixture of cumin seed and brown sugar, symbolizing willingness to share the bitter and the sweet in life together.

kalasha (kaḷaśa), rounded water vessel,

serving as an essential part of the Vedic purification rites and providing sanctified water throughout the ceremony.

Kali Yuga, fourth in the 4-yuga cycle, lasting 432,000 solar years, ending in the destruction of the world, and re-cycling of the chaturyugas.

kalpa(m), generally, a day in the life of the creator Brahma. Brahma's life covers 7 kalpas: Matsya, Kūrma, Lakshmi, Shweta Varaha, Shiva, Brahma and Vishnu Kalpa. We are now (2006) halfway through the fourth kalpa in the lifetime of the current Brahma.

Kanyadanam (Kanyādānam), ceremony of the giving away of the bride by her parents.

Kashiyatra (Kāśīyātra), the ritual journey to Varanasi (Benares).

Kāshyapa, the son of the rishi Marichi, married the 13 daughters of Daksha; he is named in the Ashirvadam to evoke the birth of many children.

Ketū, one of the Navagrahas; lunar node; Cauda Draconis; a malign influence connected with comets).

Krishna (Kṛṣṇa), avatar of Vishnu; in the epic Mahabharata he is prince of Dwaraka, a cousin of the Pandavas; he is also the charioteer who addresses Arjuna on the battlefield of Kurukshetra, delivering the Bhagavad Gita.

krishṇa paksha, dark fortnight, immediately leading into the new moon.

Krita Yuga (Kṛta Yuga), also called Satya Yuga, first in the 4-yuga cycle, lasting 432,000 x 4 = 1,728,000 solar years; an Age of Gold.

kshatriya (kṣatriya), one of the four castes, the warrior.

Kubera, Vedic lord of wealth, regent of the North; he is invoked in the Ashirvadam for the blessing of wealth and happiness.

kuladharma, family tradition.

kumkum, powder in vermillion and other shades of red used extensively in ritual ceremonies and for cosmetics.

Laaja Homa (Lāja Homa), fire ceremony in which parched rice (laaja) is offered to Agni.

loka, world: seven worlds are inhabited by gods, humans and all other celestial and terrestrial beings (Bhuloka, Bhuvarloka, Suvarloka, Maharloka, Janaloka, Tapoloka and Satyaloka). The first three, the Triloka, are invoked in rituals; they are deluged and reborn in each kalpa.

madhuparkam, sweet drink or mixture of honey and yoghurt, presented to the groom on his arrival.

Mahābhārata, second great epic of India, featuring the dynastic quarrel between the descendants of Bharata, the Kurus and the Pandavas, which becomes a war between good and evil.

Mahāganapati Pūja, a ceremony of worship offered to Ganapati by the groom and his family, the day before the wedding wishing for prevention of obstacles and a successful start to the new stage in life.

mahāyuga, a span of the 4-yuga cycle; also chaturyuga, 4.32 million solar years.

Mangala, Mars; one of the Navagrahas (Nine Planets).

mangaḷashtak, the prayers and songs recited at the time of the bride's arrival at the mantap.

Māngalyadhāranam, ceremony of the tying of the mangalasutra or tāli/thali around the bride's neck by the groom.

Mangal Phera, also Lāja Homa, in which the couple circle the fire altar four times, and the bride makes offerings of parched rice.

mantap (mandapam), sacred space prepared for the wedding, usually four pillars, often with young banana trees fastened to them, with a canopy, decorated with flower garlands and a string of mango or other leaves across the front.

Manu, mythical progenitor of the human race; 14 Manus rule over one day in the life span of Brahma; the first Manu is Svayambhuva; the current Manu is Vaivasvata.

manvantara, the reign of each Manu; = 71 mahayugas or 306,720,000 solar years.

masa/maasa (māsa), lunar month of approximately 29.5 days; there are 12 lunar or solar months in the year:
1. Chaitra (March-April);
2. Vaishakha (April-May);
3. Jyeshta (May-June);
4. āshādha (June-July);
5. Shrāvana (July-August);
6. Bhādrapada (August-September);
7. āshvayuja (September-October);
8. Kārthika (October-November);
9. Mārgasheera (November-December)
10. Pushya (December-January);
11. Māgha (January-February);
12. Phālguni (February-March).

The names here are given in Sanskrit. Certain months are considered less auspicious for wedding ceremonies: āshādh, Bhadrapad, and Shunya (the month added to the lunar year every 30 months to bring it in line with the solar year, the adhika māsa).

mehndi, henna; a powder made from the leaves of the henna plant are used to create elaborate decorative patterns on the hands and feet of the bride, and her friends, usually the day before the wedding (See Appendix 5, Makeup).

Milni, means meeting, often called Swagatam or greeting; refers to the ceremonial meeting between the groom and his family and the bride's family at a point outside the bride's home or wedding venue which begins the main ceremony.

Mitra, Vedic god; Friendship; social bond. Sometime associated with the sun.

Mṛkanda, father of the rishi Markandaya, is recalled in the Ashirvadam as an example of longevity.

muhūrtam, an auspicious time range selected by a qualified priest or person versed in the sacred calendar to be the best interval for beginning or performing the highlights in a wedding or other sacred rite.

nakshatra, constellation; 27 Nakshatras are contained in the Zodiac, at 13.20 degrees each. Horoscopes are based on the position of the moon in a particular nakshatra at birth.

Nala and Damayanti, an ideal couple, named in the Ashiravadam; their story is told in the epic Mahabharata.

Navagrahas, the Nine Planets of Vedic astrology: Surya (Sun); Chandra (Moon); Angāraka or Mangala (Mars); Budha (Mercury); Brhaspati or Guru (Jupiter); Shukra (Venus); Shani (Saturn); Rahu (lunar node; eclipse); Ketu (lunar node; comet).

Oonjal (Ūnjal), a South Indian custom in which the bride and groom sit in a swing.

pāda, part of Brahma's day; Prathama pāda is the first part of Dvitīya parārdha (the second half) of Brahma's life.

Pādaprakshālana, ritual washing of the groom's feet.

paksha (pakṣa), fortnight, defined by the prevailing phase of the moon: either the bright fortnight or two-week period ending with the full moon (Shukla Paksha), or the dark fortnight (Krishna Paksha) leading to the new moon.

para, half the life-span of Brahma.

parārdha, half a para.

pativrata, a devoted and virtuous wife, for example, the wives of the sages as evoked in the Ashirvadam. See *Saptarishi*.

pooja (pūja), ceremony of worship.

poornima (pūrṇima), full moon.

Pradhāna Homa, principal fire ceremony, observed first at a fire ritual.

Prajāpati, lord of progeny.

praḷaya, chaotic floods which engulf the Three Worlds (Triloka) at the end of each kalpa.

Pravara, recital of the spiritual lineage of the bride and groom, usually accompanied by recital of their ancestry going back three generations.

Pundareekaaksha (Pundarīkākṣa), epithet of Vishnu, i.e. the lotus-eyed.

purāṇa, a story poem or collection of stories which covers creation, destruction and recreation/salvation of the world, centered around the saga of a principal god or avatar and royal house, and the history, customs and beliefs of the age.

Purandara, a name of Indra. Spouse: Sachi.

Rahu (Rāhu), one of the Navagrahas; lunar node; Caput Draconis; a malign influence connected with eclipses.

Rāhukalam, a period of time each day which is considered inauspicious for beginning a rite. Rahu, in Hindu legend is a snake which swallows the sun; in astrology it marks a path of intersection of the sun and moon, the north lunar node, during which eclipses occur. (See Rahukalam, Appendix III)

Raibhī, ritual verse (Griffith footnote to *RV*, 10. 85. 6).

Rakshā Bandhana, ceremony in which turmeric-tinted threads are tied around the right wrists of bride and groom to signify that they are taking part in a rite, and for protection.

Rama/Raama(Rāma), hero of the Ramayana, prince of Ayodhya; avatar of Vishnu.

Rakshā Visarjana, ceremony of removing the raksha thread.

rāshis, signs of the Zodiac:

1. Maisha (Aries) Ram;
2. Vrushabha (Taurus) Bull;
3. Mithuna (Gemini) Couple;
4. Karka (Cancer) Crab;
5. Simha (Leo) Lion;
6. Kanya (Virgo) Maiden;
7. Tula (Libra) Scales;
8. Vrushchika (Scorpio) Scorpion;
9. Dhanu (Saggitarius) Bow;
10. Makar (Capricorn) Sea Monster;
11. Kumbha (Aquarius) Pot;
12. Meena (Pisces) Fish.

Rig (ṛg) Veda, the oldest of the four Vedas. Mandala X, Hymn LXXXV contains the reference to the bridal of Suryā, daughter of the sun, to Soma, the moon, in lines which are still used in modern Vedic wedding rituals.

ritu or rutu (ṛtu), season; the 6 seasons of the 12 lunar months in the year: Vasanta (Spring); Greeshma (Summer); Varsha (Monsoon); Sharad (Autumn); Hemanta (Winter); Shishira (Dewy)

samskāra, Hindu rite of passage; 16 in all, of which marriage is one.

samvatsara, the Vedic year; these repeat in a cycle of 60 (see Samvatsara Table, Appendix IV).

sankalpa (samkalpam), ritual declaration of place and time for a religious rite, as in a wedding ceremony.

Sanskrit (Samskrit), oldest extant Indo-European language, related to the oldest classical languages of Europe, Latin and Greek; it is now mostly liturgical, especially the Vedic Sanskrit used in wedding rituals; the many modern languages of North India (Hindi, Marathi, Bengali, etc.) have developed mainly from Prakrits, less formal regional derivations from Sanskrit.

sanyās, the life of the renunciate, the last of the four stages of life.

Saptapadi, (also Hindi. *Sapta Padi)*, the seven steps taken together, by the couple with the groom leading the bride, either around the fire once, or, near it while she steps into seven circles or seven mounds of rice, according to family tradition. Each step is taken with a purpose. After the seventh step, the marriage is legally ratified, by law, according to the Manava Dharma Shastra and the Hindu Code Bill.

Sapta Rishi (Saptarṣi), the constellation (L. Ursa Major; Big Dipper); also the Seven Sages of legend. The sages' names may differ in the separate scriptures and other writings which refer to the constellation. The rishis (and their wives) mentioned in the Ashirvadam as examples of ideal couples are: Kashyapa (and his thirteen wives), Agastya (and Lopamudra), Atri (and Anasuya), Gautama (and Ahalya), Rishyashringa (and Shanta), Vasishta (and Arundhati). The father of rishi Markandaya is included as a type of longevity.

Sāshtānga, ceremony in which the couple bend down to touch the feet of elders in the family, to be blessed, at the end of the rite.

Saubhāgyavatībhava, ceremony in which married ladies bless the bride.

Saubhari, sage whose name is mentioned in the Ashirvadam, together with his wives, in a blessing for the birth of healthy children.

Savitar (Savitr), sun.

shringar (śṛingar), female adornments, usually in the many forms of jewelry, flowers, and traditional makeup which were used to beautify the bride (See Appendix V); this has often taken the part of a separate ceremony or party for ladies; the application of mehndi is included here.

shukla paksha (śukla pakṣa), the bright fortnight, ending with the full moon day.

Shukra, Venus; one of the Navagrahas; preceptor of the asuras (titans).

Shunya (śūnya), literally zero; adhika māsa; the extra month added to the lunar year every three years; not considered auspicious for weddings.

shodashopacharas (śodaśopacārās), the 16 traditional methods of worship.

sindhoor (sindhūr), auspicious red powder used by married women to apply the bindu or tika (round forehead mark); also used by her groom to mark the hair parting of the bride.

Sita/Seeta(Sītā), heroine of the Ramayana, faithful wife of Rama.

Soma, Vedic god of the moon and of plants; his wedding to Suryā, daughter of the sun, in the Rig Veda, provides many of the earliest wedding-related verses still in use.

Sūrya, the sun.

Suryaa/Sooryaa (Sūryā), daughter of the sun.

Swagatam (Svāgatam), the ceremonial greeting of the groom and his entourage, including his family, in which he is garlanded, and honored by the bride's family.

***Shweta Varaha** Kalpa* (śvētavarāha), the current, fourth kalpa in Brahma's life-span; the White Boar's time, in which, according to legend, Lord Varaha (an incarnation of Vishnu) emerged from Brahma in the form of of a white boar in order to rescue the earth from the bottom of the cosmic ocean after a flood.

Talambraalu (Talambrālu), regional custom from Andhra Pradesh in which the bride and groom pour rice over each other in a playful mode.

tali (tāḷi), wedding pendant, equivalent to a mangalasutra

thali (thāli), metallic plate or tray; also a wedding pendant .

tithi, lunar day, the time taken by the moon to move 12 degrees from the sun. When the sun and moon are at the same longitude, it is amavasya (new moon); when they are 180 degrees apart, it is full moon (Pūrnima). There are 30 tithis in each lunar month, 15 in each paksha.

Treta Yuga, second in the yuga cycle, lasting 432,000 x 3 = 1,296,000 years.

Triloka, also Trailokya, the three worlds: Bhuloka (Earth), Antariksha Loka (Cosmos), and Dyuloka/ Devaloka or Swarga (Heaven); these are the material worlds, accessible to humans, and all creatures as well as gods, which are destroyed and remade in each kalpa.

turmeric, see ***haldi***.

uttarayana (uttarāyana), northward course of the sun; cited in a sankalpam.

vaasara (vāsara), day of the week; named after the first 7 navagrahas:

1. Indu vāsara (Sunday);
2. Soma vāsara (Monday);
3. Mangala vāsara (Tuesday);
4. Budha vāsara (Wednesday);
5. Guru vāsara (Thursday);
6. Shukra vāsara (Friday);
7. Shani vāsara (Saturday)

Vara Pūja, ceremony in which the groom is honored by the bride's father as a personification of Vishnu.

Varuṇa, Vedic lord of waters and of destiny; regent of the west.

Veda (Vēda), one of four books which form the bedrock of Hinduism or Sanatana Dharma: Rig Veda, Yajur Veda, Sama Veda, and Atharva Veda.

Vedic, pertaining to Hindu religious rites; to the historic period (dating still to be decided), the language (early Sanskrit) and literature, the culture, and beliefs derived from the Vedas.

Vidaī, ceremony of leave-taking when the bride is about to depart for her new home.

Viśvavāsu, the Gandharva named in the Rig Veda as guardian of the bride in her home before marriage.

Vivāha, wedding, as ceremony or a samskara (one of the 16 rites of passage for a Hindu).

Yagnopavītam (yajnopavītam), the "thread ceremony" by which a brahmin (by tradition) or other Hindu who has studied the Vedas attains the status of "twice-born." At the time of marriage, the thread needs to be renewed and doubled in a separate ceremony.

yaksha (yakśa), woodland spirit.

Yama, Lord of the dead, of ancestors; Justice; regent of the south.

Yudhishtira (Yudhiṣṭhira), hero of the epic Mahabharata, eldest of the five Pandava brothers, renowned for his adherence to dharma.

Yuga, an age or era in the history of the world:
Krita Yuga or Satya Yuga: 432,000 x 4 years;
Treta Yuga: 432,000 x 3 years;
Dvapara Yuga: 432,000 x 2 years;
Kali Yuga: 432,000 years
The 4 ages collectively are called a chaturyuga, a period of 4,320,000 years. They have been popularly referred to as Ages of Gold, Silver, Bronze and Iron, with each age manifesting a deterioration in dharma or strength of moral values, intellect and physical wellbeing. As in many time periods tied to Vedic astrology, different traditions ascribe variations in these measurements. The best known has been provided above.

NOTE: Most of the above terms are transcribed from languages with differing alphabets. Over the years the best known among them have been spelled (or misspelled) in varying ways. For the sake of accuracy the international system of diacritical marks has been used in the longer ritual Sanskrit sequences and the terms in parentheses in the Glossary. However, for the general reader's comfort, these are included only where obvious in the general text and appendices. We have reverted in many cases, especially for personal and place names, to familiar usage. The general attempt has been to balance accuracy with ease of use, even when there might be a small loss in consistency.

Acknowledgements

It is with great pleasure and gratitude that I would like to thank Swami Anubhavanandaji for his gracious remarks and encouragement in the foreword. My very special thanks go to my wife Kamla, for her research contributions and usual meticulous editing.

It is a pleasure to acknowledge photographers who permitted the use of some of the photos they had taken at weddings the author performed: Gary Allen Photography, Rocio Honigmann and Joe Madri, Agahuda Khanii, Cindy Patrick, Capture the Moment Photography by Grace Cribbins, Lynn Norgren Photography, A. Vincent Scarano, George Hartzell, Jay Sheth, and Shirley Speer. And thanks to the individuals who sent the pictures taken by them and/or family friends: Roger Cole, Swarna & Dr. N.N. Raghuvir, Parashar Patel, Margot Mindich, Daya Patel, Thakorbhai Patel, V.R. Garimalla, Janine & Sunjay Patil, Sapna Gupta, Arun Basu, Praveen & Radhika Ramamurthy, Madhuri Gogineni, Aditi Saxena and Kavita & Rahul Panke.

Grateful thanks are due to our friends at GRC Direct: Sushma and Arvind Gupta, for their encouragement and support, and to Kirk Heydt for his interest and technical assistance.

Dr. Sheenu Srinivasan
Glastonbury, CT
November 2010

About the Author

Dr. Amrutur Venkatachar Srinivasan, was born in India in the village of Amrutur, Kunigal Taluk, in the southern state of Karnataka, India. He had eight years of formal education in Sanskrit, the liturgical language of Hinduism, followed by many years in the U.S. performing a wide variety of Hindu religious ceremonies of worship, weddings, housewarmings, and bhajans or kirtans.

His publication, ***The Vedic Wedding: Origins, Tradition and Practice***, (Periplus Line LLC, 2006, www.periplusbooks.com) is widely acclaimed and won the **USA Book News 2007 Best Book Award** in the category of Eastern Religions. He has developed a contemporary format for Vedic (Hindu) weddings which retains all essential Vedic rites within a one to two hour ceremony, and in practice has blended this approach with those of other creeds in many interfaith weddings. See www.indianweddings.us.com

He is a popular writer and speaker, and has published/presented numerous papers on a variety of cultural, social and religious issues in the U.S. and India. He has given courses on the classical literature of India at the University of Connecticut and Wesleyan University. Founding member of the Connecticut Valley Hindu Temple Society, he also established the Raga Club of Connecticut in 2006. The current publication *Hindu Wedding: A Guide* retains the Vedic ceremony in full detail as before, with some revision -- in convenient paperback format.

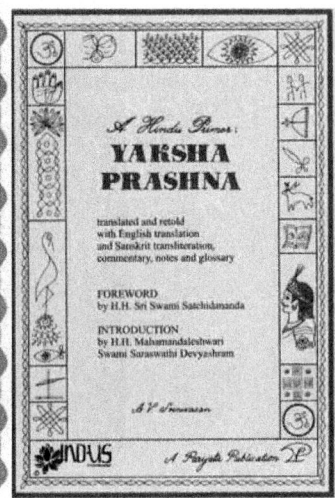

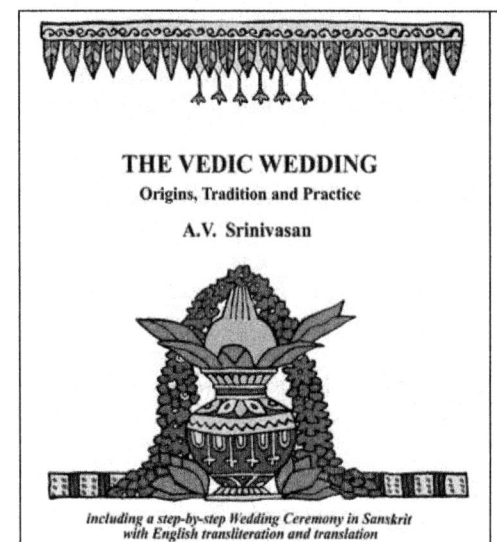

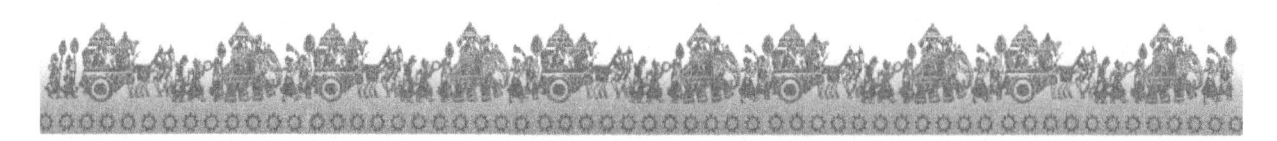

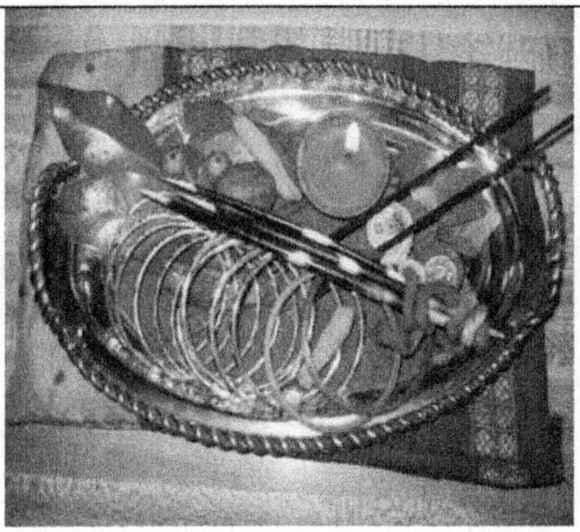

The Vedic ceremony, known as सीमतं (Sīmantam) or सीमंतोन्नयन

(Sīmantōnnayana), a prenatal ceremony, is one of the samskaras (Hindi: sanskar) or rites of passage prescribed for Hindus. It involves purification and protective rites aimed at assuring a safe birth of a baby while cheering and felicitating the mother-to-be.

In Gujarat and some parts of Northern India, this ceremony is also known as Shrimant, Khodo Bharavo or Godh Bharai, and principally involves filling the lap of the mother-to-be with symbols of prosperity as will be discussed later. It is a ceremony scheduled to be performed during the later part of the pregnancy and is usually done only once, during the first pregnancy.

Just as the wind … ruffles a pool of lotuses,
so smoothly shall the baby be stirred into birth

Transliteration Scheme

अ	आ	इ	ई	उ	ऊ	ऋ	ॠ	ए	ए	ऐ
a	ā	i	ī	u	ū	r̥	r̥̄	e	ē	ai

ओ	ओ	औ	अं	अः
o	ō	au	am	a:

क	ख	ग	घ	ङ
ka	kha	ga	gha	ń
च	छ	ज	झ	ञ
ca	cha	ja	jha	ñ
ट	ठ	ड	ढ	ण
ṭ	ṭha	ḍ	ḍh	ṇa
त	थ	द	ध	न
ta	tha	da	dha	na
प	फ	ब	भ	म
pa	pha	ba	bha	ma

य	र	ल	व	स	श	ष	ह	ळ
ya	ra	la	va	sa	śa	ṣa	ha	l̥

Key for Baraha Script

a A i I u U Ru RU
e E ai o O au aM aH

Alternatively
A or aa, U or uu, etc.
may also be used.

Brief Guide to Pronunciation: **a** = u in hut, **ī** = ee, **u** = u in put, **ū** = oo in tool,
e = e in they, **c** = ch in cheese, **ń** = ng, **ñ** = ny, ṇ= (r)n, ṭ = as in ton,
ḍ = as in dog, **tha** and **dha** as for ṭ and ḍ with tongue tip rolled back, **ś** = as in shun, ṣ = as in shine,
r̥ = French r, r̥̄ = previous r held longer**;** **h** in aspirated letters must be sounded, eg: **kh** as in rock-hard;
jn = gn (g is sounded)

Puja Booklets published by the author

www.periplusbooks.com

CPSIA information can be obtained
at www.ICGtesting.com
Printed in the USA
BVOW08s0715070218
507493BV00006B/248/P

9 781935 052388